The Voice
of the Turtle

Also by John van Druten

PLAYS

Young Woodley   The Distaff Side

Diversion   Flowers of the Forest

After All   Most of the Game

London Wall   Gertie Maude

There's Always Juliet   Leave Her to Heaven

Somebody Knows   Old Acquaintance

Behold, We Live   The Damask Cheek
                                 (*with Lloyd Morris*)

NOVELS

Young Woodley   And Then You Wish

A Woman on Her Way

AUTOBIOGRAPHY

The Way to the Present

The Voice
of the Turtle

A COMEDY IN THREE ACTS

BY

John van Druten

DRAMATISTS PLAY SERVICE · NEW YORK

COPYRIGHT, 1943, 1944, BY JOHN VAN DRUTEN

Published simultaneously in Canada by
The Macmillan Company of Canada Limited

MANUFACTURED IN THE UNITED STATES OF AMERICA

To DELLY

appreciatively

THE VOICE OF THE TURTLE *was first presented by Alfred de Liagre, Jr., at the Shubert Theatre, New Haven, Conn., on November 4, 1943, and at the Morosco Theatre, New York City, on December 8, 1943, with the following cast:*

SALLY MIDDLETON	Margaret Sullavan
OLIVE LASHBROOKE	Audrey Christie
BILL PAGE	Elliott Nugent

STAGED by John van Druten
SETTING by Stewart Chaney

SCENES

ACT ONE

SCENE I. Friday afternoon

SCENE II. Friday evening

ACT TWO

SCENE I. Saturday morning

SCENE II. Late Saturday night

ACT THREE

SCENE I. Sunday morning

SCENE II. Late Sunday afternoon

The action, throughout, takes place over a week-end in early April in an apartment in the East Sixties, near Third Avenue, New York City.

Act One

ACT ONE

THE SCENE *throughout is a smallish apartment in New York, in the East Sixties, near Third Avenue. The set comprises the entire apartment, with the exception of the bathroom. We see the bedroom, with double bed, to the right of the stage; living room center; kitchen, through a swing-door, left. The kitchen has an icebox, stove and sink in a combined unit in the left wall. The front door to the apartment is in the back wall, center, opening into the living room, which is down two steps. The windows are in the right wall of the bedroom, back wall of living room, and back wall of kitchen. Under the living-room window is a day-bed, disguised as a couch. The telephone is below the bed in the bedroom. The bathroom and dressing room are off right of the back wall of the bedroom.*

SCENE I

The apartment, late in the afternoon of a Friday at the beginning of April.

When the curtain rises, SALLY MIDDLETON *is discovered in the kitchen, fixing a tray of drinks which she carries into the living room through the swing-door. She sets the tray down on a table, muttering to herself as she does so. Actually, she is running over the words of the Potion Scene from* Romeo and Juliet, *but only becomes audible as she reaches the end.* SALLY *is twenty-two, small, direct, naive and very pretty.*

3

SALLY

(Finishing the speech aloud)

Stay, Tybalt, stay! Romeo, I come!

> *(She pushes open the swing-door again, returning to the kitchen)*

This do I drink to thee!

> *(Then in her own voice)*

There, I know it!

> *(She opens the icebox and gets out the tray of ice cubes. During the ensuing business, she starts the Potion Scene again, acting it to herself, and not overdoing it; the only thing that makes it ridiculous is the business that punctuates it)*

Farewell!

> *(Slams icebox door)*

God knows when we shall meet again!
I have a faint, cold fear thrills through my veins—

> *(Turns on the hot faucet to run over the ice tray)*

That almost freezes up the heat of life.
I'll call them back again to comfort me.

> *(Ice breaks into sink. She turns off tap)*

Nurse! What should she do here?
My dismal scene I needs must act alone.
Come, vial.

> *(Takes up ice-bucket, and starts to pick up ice)*

What if this mixture do not work at all?
Shall I be married then tomorrow morning?
No, no, this shall forbid it.

> *(Looks around for a prop, sees mixing spoon and uses it)*

Lie thou there!

> *(She places the spoon on the drain-board, then takes the ice-bucket into the living room, where she puts it on the drink-table, still reciting)*

What if it be a poison which the friar

4

Subtly have ministered to have me dead . . .
> (*She dries up*)

Have me dead . . . have me dead . . .
> (*She crosses to the couch where a Temple Shakespeare is lying open, and refreshes her memory*)

Lest in this marriage he should be dishonor'd,
Because he married me before to Romeo.
> (*Front-door buzzer rings. She goes to answer it, gabbling the next lines*)

I fear it is, and yet methinks it should not,
For he hath still been tried a holy . . .
> (*She opens the door.* OLIVE LASHBROOKE *is standing outside. She is about twenty-eight, smart and attractive, without being good-looking, and rather gay*)

Olive!

OLIVE

Sally! Darling!
> (*They kiss.*)

SALLY

Come in. How are you?

OLIVE

Couldn't be better. (*Looks around*) So this is it! It's very grand.

SALLY

> (*Pleased*)

Do you think so?

OLIVE

Very. How long have you had it?

SALLY

Six weeks.

OLIVE

(*Inspecting; impressed*)

Um!

SALLY

(*Naively excited*)

Do you want to see it all?

OLIVE

Sure.

SALLY

Well, this is the living room. It's sunken. Kitchen's in here.
(*Opens door. They go through.*)

OLIVE

Darling, it's enormous! You could feed the whole army. Do you have a maid?

SALLY

Colored. Daily. *When* she comes. Which isn't very often. I think she's got a complicated love life.

OLIVE

Don't we all? (*They return to living room*) How did you find this?

SALLY

It's Claire Henley's. Claire's on the road with the Lunts.

OLIVE

(*As they re-cross living room*)

I don't know how that girl gets the break she does. I was sick about *your* show. Did you get my message, opening night?

SALLY

Yes, I didn't know where to thank you. You were jumping around so.

OLIVE

Darling, I *know*. Split weeks and one-night stands. It's heaven to be through. How long did you run, actually?

SALLY

Five days.

OLIVE

Did you get any notices?

SALLY

A couple of mentions. (*Opening bedroom door*) Here's the bedroom.

OLIVE

(*Going in*)

Very saucy. (*Flippantly*) Luxe.

SALLY

What?

OLIVE

(*As before*)

Luxe. French, darling. One of those untranslatable expressions. It means luxury. And beds like that!

SALLY

(*Pointing off*)

Bathroom and dressing room in there.

7

OLIVE

(*Impressed*)

Dressing room! (*She peeps in.*)

SALLY

(*Excusing it*)

Well . . .

OLIVE

Darling, it's the cutest place I ever saw in all my life. (*Going to the window*) Where do you look out?

SALLY

Onto the summer garden of the "Bonne Chanson." That French restaurant next door.

OLIVE

What's that like?

SALLY

Lovely. But terribly expensive. You know, no menu. The man just comes and *suggests*.

OLIVE

Put yourself right next door to temptation, eh? Or is it for the boy-friends when they come to take you out? (*Acting*) "Where shall we eat?" "Wherever you say." "How about the place next door?" "Okay." (*Back to her own voice*) I know. I once thought of taking an apartment over the Colony, myself. What are you paying Claire for this?

SALLY

(*Slightly embarrassed*)

A hundred and a quarter.

OLIVE

Have you got another job?

SALLY

No.

OLIVE

No! And there's nothing in the offing, this late in the season, for any of us.

SALLY

I know. But I still have a little money left over from that radio serial I did. And it's when you're out of work you *need* a nice place to live. When you're *in* work . . .

OLIVE

You live at Sardi's—if you can get in. Yes, but all the same! What did you want to move for, anyway?

SALLY

I was tired of a hotel-room. And there were reasons.

OLIVE

(*Eagerly*)

What?

SALLY

(*Evasively*)

Not now. Come and have a drink.

OLIVE

Lovely.
(*They return to the living room.*)

9

SALLY

(*As they go*)

What'll you have?

OLIVE

What have you got?

SALLY

Whatever you want. Gin . . . rum . . . Scotch . . .

OLIVE

Scotch? You *have* been on a bust. (*Flippantly*) Or is all this
. . . guilty splendor?

SALLY

Don't be silly. Scotch?

OLIVE

Sure. (SALLY *pours two Scotches. A large one for* OLIVE, *and
a smaller one for herself.* OLIVE *picks up the Shakespeare*) What
on earth are you studying Juliet for?

SALLY

(*Pouring*)

Practice.

OLIVE

Darling, you're out of your mind. You know, you take the
theatre too seriously. You'll be going to Madame Pushkin's school
next, studying "de free body," and learning how to act *milk!*
(*Breaking off*) I had the greatest success telling about Madame
Pushkin in the company, by the way. Henry Atherton adored
her. I gave you credit for inventing her.

SALLY

(*Bringing her the drink*)

Was it wonderful playing with Henry Atherton? I've always had the most terrific thing about him. You used to have, too.

OLIVE

Did I? Well, it's gone now, if I did. He isn't interested in anything a day over twenty. There was a little ingenue in the company—she couldn't have been more than eighteen. You've never seen such carryings-on . . . holding hands and giggling in the wings, all through my one decent scene.

SALLY

(*Disappointed*)

Oh!

OLIVE

(*Drinking*)

It's good to be back in New York. By the way, I've asked someone to call for me here. Is that all right?

SALLY

Of course. Who is it?

OLIVE

A man called Bill Page.

SALLY

An actor?

OLIVE

No, just a man. At least, he used to be. He's a soldier now. He's at Camp Something-or-Other up the Hudson. Got a week-end

pass, starting this afternoon. I left a message at my hotel telling
him to come on here and pick me up.

SALLY

What's he like?

OLIVE

He's sweet. And he's mine!

SALLY

I didn't mean . . .

OLIVE

I know, darling, but I thought I'd tell you. I've known him
for ages. He used to live in Pittsburgh, and whenever I played
there we always had a "gay little something." Though when I
say "whenever," I think actually it was only twice. I'd lost sight
of him for years, and then when we were in Detroit about six
weeks ago, he turned up again. He was stationed somewhere
near, and came to see the show. Now, he's moved up here.

SALLY

(*Smiling*)

And are you still having a "gay little something"?

OLIVE

Well, we did in Detroit.

SALLY

Are you in love with him?

12

OLIVE

No, darling, not a bit. But he's attractive. Only he's sort of the
. . . reserved kind. You never know what he's thinking, or get
any further with him.

SALLY

It doesn't sound as though there was much further left for you
to get. (*Rises*) By the way, what's happened to the Commander?

OLIVE

Ned Burling? Ah, darling, now you're talking! He's at sea
somewhere . . . I guess. What makes you ask about him?

SALLY

I was just remembering *that* "gay little something" of yours.

OLIVE

And it *was* something!

SALLY

Do you ever hear from him?

OLIVE

No, he's not the writing kind. He was . . . you know . . .
just "Butch." Besides, that was one of those . . . (*Mocking*)
"lovely things that isn't meant to last. A little Intermezzo, or a
wild, brief gypsy Czardas." Ah, me! Quel goings-on!

SALLY

(*Moving away, repeating the phrase, reflectively*)
"One of those lovely things that isn't meant to last."

13

OLIVE

(*Catching her tone, crosses to her*)

Sally, what's the matter? You're unhappy about something. What is it? Is it . . . love?

SALLY

I guess so. If you can call it that.

OLIVE

You can always call it that. Come on. Tell Auntie Olive all about it. Well?

SALLY

Well, you've heard of Kenneth Bartlett—the producer?

OLIVE

Yes. Darling, it isn't *him?* (SALLY *nods*) Sally, how simply sensational! And he's putting on *Romeo and Juliet* for you!

SALLY

Don't be silly. You know he only does musicals.

OLIVE

Yes, the new one opened last night. It's a smash, from the notices. Where did you meet him?

SALLY

At a cocktail party. (*She stops.*)

OLIVE

(*Eagerly*)

Well, go on. Tell.

14

SALLY

(*Slowly*)

Well, he's terribly nice. And young, and attractive. At least, I guess he's around forty, but he seemed young. And we talked . . . about the theatre, of course . . . and then he took me on to dinner. We went next door. That was the first time I'd been there.

OLIVE

But not the last.

SALLY

(*Shyly*)

No. It sort of became . . . "our" place.

OLIVE

How long ago was all this?

SALLY

Two months. His show was in rehearsal, then. He told me all about it . . . sang me some of the songs. He made me feel wonderful . . . like being starred, and getting the star dressing room. Do you know?

OLIVE

I know.

SALLY

Well, then I found that Claire was going away, and had this place right next door to . . .

OLIVE

"Your" place . . .

15

SALLY

So I took it. You know, it was funny . . . when I came to see it, Claire had the radio on, and it was playing the Londonderry Air. That's always been my lucky tune. I thought it meant the apartment would be lucky.

OLIVE

So you let her soak you a hundred and a quarter.

SALLY

Well, it was nice to have. And . . . (*Timidly*) just occasionally he stayed all night . . . and I got breakfast, and . . . oh, I don't know . . . but it was nice. I love having someone to do for. Even in that tiny hotel room . . . that time *you* stayed with me, because of the snow, do you remember? . . . It was sort of exciting, like having "Cousin Olive" to stay overnight when one was little. (*Pointing below window*) By the way, if you ever want it, that's a day-bed.

OLIVE

Lovely. But what happened with "Cousin Bartlett"? What went wrong?

SALLY

(*Grimly*)

I did.

OLIVE

Yes, I know, dear. But what went wrong?

SALLY

Well, he talked a lot about keeping it *gay* . . . not bringing love into it . . . or getting serious about each other . . .

16

OLIVE

And *you* did, and he didn't like that?

SALLY

He said I made scenes.

OLIVE

Did you?

SALLY

I guess I did. At least, they wouldn't be scenes if they were in a play, but . . . yes, I guess I made scenes. Little ones. You see, he's married.

OLIVE

Did you know that?

SALLY

Yes, he told me that the first evening. But they don't get on, and she's a lot older than he is. Oh, *he* didn't tell me that. He didn't say anything about her, except to let me know he *had* a wife. And they've two children, so you see, it couldn't be anything serious for *him*. Oh, he was very sweet about it . . . really he was. Only he said that it couldn't go on like that . . . for *my* sake. So, it's all over. We said good-bye a month ago. (*Rising and starting to pace*) I've been so miserable ever since. We've had the most awful weather. I don't think spring's *ever* coming, this year. I've just stayed home, and studied *Juliet* and read Dorothy Parker's poems. I never used to mind being by myself, but now . . . since Ken . . . Well, it's the first time I've had an apartment of my own, and it seems such waste.

OLIVE

I know. I feel the same way whenever I go to a hotel, and they give me a big double room all to myself.

17

SALLY

Oh, what did I have to go and fall in love for? Or, if I did, why did I have to go and show it? Or, worse still, talk about it? I believe there's nothing men hate so much as talking about it.

OLIVE

There's nothing they hate so much as *your* talking about it.

SALLY

Well, it's not going to happen again. Sex, I mean. Not for a long, long time. Not till I'm thirty. It should never have started in the first place. Father was quite right about the theatre.

OLIVE

Oh, darling, you're not going to start blaming it on the theatre?

SALLY

If I'd stayed home in Joplin, none of this would have happened.

OLIVE

Don't they . . . in Joplin?

SALLY

Olive, tell me something. Something I want to know.

OLIVE

What?

SALLY

Well, *do* ordinary girls? I was raised to think they didn't. Didn't even want to. And what I want to know is—don't they?

They don't in movies. Oh, I know that's censorship . . . but . . . the people who go and *see* the movies . . . are they like that too? Or else don't they notice that it's all false?

OLIVE

I've wondered about that, myself.

SALLY

Even in Shakespeare, his heroines don't. Ever. Juliet carries on like crazy about not. I don't know whether what Mother and Father taught me was right, or true, or anything. Were you raised like that?

OLIVE

Oh, sure. And I wasn't even legitimate. But Mama raised me just as strict as if I was.

SALLY

Did you have qualms when you started?

OLIVE

Never.

SALLY

What did you feel?

OLIVE

I just felt—"So, this is it! I like it!" (*Then, kindly*) Oh, Sally, darling, you're not starting a conscience, or thinking you're promiscuous, because you've had one affair, are you?

SALLY

(*Unhappily*)

I've had two. There was that boy in the company at Skowhegan last summer that I was so unhappy about. I told you.

19

OLIVE

Well, two, then.

SALLY

No, I . . . don't think I'm promiscuous . . . yet. Though I don't imagine anyone ever does think that about themselves. Do . . . (*She stops.*)

OLIVE

Do *I* . . . were you going to say?

SALLY

Well, I was, only I suddenly realized how awful it sounded.

OLIVE

No, I don't. Maybe you're right, and no one does, but I just think for a gal with a funny face, I've really done rather well. *You're* pretty. You can afford to be choosey. (*Walking away*) I wonder what's happened to Bill. I hope they gave him the message. Would you mind if I called up the hotel to ask?

SALLY

No, do. It's in the bedroom. Can I fix you another drink?

OLIVE

(*Nodding*)

A tiny one. (*She goes into bedroom, where she dials a number on the telephone.*)

SALLY

I'll just get a glass for *him*. (*She goes into kitchen, and gets a third glass, then comes back and fixes a drink for* OLIVE.)

20

OLIVE

(*In bedroom, on phone*)

Give me the desk, please. Hello, desk? This is Miss Lash-brooke. Has a Sergeant Page called for me? I left a note . . . Oh, he did? How long ago? Oh, thank you. By the way, you might just see if there are any messages for me. I'll hold on. (SALLY *comes into the bedroom. To* SALLY) He's on his way here.

SALLY

Good. (*Hands* OLIVE *her glass.*)

OLIVE

Thanks. (*Drinks. Then, into phone*) Hello . . . yes . . . yes . . . I see . . . all right, just leave it in my box. Anything else? Who called? (*Her voice rising in excitement*) Lieutenant Comm . . . *what* number? Wait a minute, I'll get a pencil. (*She gets one from the telephone table, scribbling on a pad*) Give me that number again. Eldorado . . . yes . . . What time was that? Thanks. (*She hangs up, and sits staring.*)

SALLY

Was that *the* Commander?

OLIVE

(*A little dazed and excited. Nods*)

He's in town. He called at five o'clock. I must call him. (SALLY *starts to leave*) Don't go. (*Lifts receiver and dials*) Wouldn't you know it would happen like this? Well, at least he called me. That's something.

SALLY

(*Sits on bed, staring at her*)

You're still crazy about him, aren't you?

OLIVE

Yes, damn it. In the worst way.

SALLY

Well, don't let him know it.

OLIVE

(*Laughing with slight bitterness*)

You—giving *me* advice now! (*Into phone*) Hello . . . is Commander Burling there? Ned? This is Olive. Yes, I just called the hotel and they told me. When did you get into town? You did? You are? When? You mean, you're just here till . . . Well, I never got it. I've been on the road with a play, and I guess the mail got . . . Oh, I can't. I'm terribly sorry, but I can't. How about lunch tomorrow? (*Disappointed*) Oh. No, I'm tied up the whole week-end. I've got someone to look after. Yes, I know. Darling, I know. I know, but . . . (*She is growing agonized*) Oh, hell, I will! Yes, yes, I will. I don't know how I . . . but I will. What's the time now? Oh, my God, no, no, make it eight, will you? Eight at my hotel. Yes . . . lovely to talk to *you*. Good-bye now. (*She hangs up, and looks at* SALLY) There. There's an object lesson in how not to act with a man.

SALLY

You're seeing him tonight?

OLIVE

It's his last leave. He's got till Sunday afternoon. And he called *me* right away. He wrote to me! I'm going to dinner with him. (*She rises.*)

SALLY

But . . . What about . . . *this* one? (*Pointing to front door.*)

22

OLIVE

I don't know. I must think. What am I going to do? Bill's on his way here. Sally, what am I going to say?

SALLY

(*Unhelpfully*)

I don't know.

OLIVE

No, but be some help.

SALLY

I can't. Why did you have to have dinner with him? You could have met him later . . . say, for supper.

OLIVE

And let Bill spend the whole evening . . . "expecting"? That's the kind of thing men never forgive. No, this way, he'll at least have a chance to fix up something else for himself. Could I say that my family . . .? No, he knows I haven't any. Besides, one can always ditch one's family after midnight. Who *can't* one ditch? That's what it comes down to. Who can't one ditch? Mother . . . father . . . brother . . . grandmother. (*Suddenly*) I've got it. Husband!

SALLY

Whose husband?

OLIVE

Mine!

SALLY

Doesn't he know you haven't a husband?

23

OLIVE

He hasn't seen me for about two years. Except that flash in Detroit . . . and that wasn't the kind of occasion when one would mention being married. And now my husband's turned up on his last leave. . . .

SALLY

(*Slightly shocked*)

Olive, you can't!

OLIVE

I've got to tell him *something*. Oh, darling, I know it's awful of me, but you've not seen Ned. It's nearly a year since I have, and he's so divine. (*Front-door buzzer sounds*) There *is* Bill. Listen, you'll help me?

SALLY

How?

OLIVE

With the husband story.

SALLY

I'll slip out, and let you talk to him.

OLIVE

No, don't do that. Stay and back me up.

SALLY

I couldn't.

OLIVE

I would . . . for you.
(*Buzzer again.*)

24

SALLY

I *must* answer the door.

OLIVE

(*As they go into living room*)

What's the time?

SALLY

A quarter of seven.

OLIVE

Oh, my God, and I've got to be dressed by eight. Why do things like this always have to happen to me?

SALLY

Shall I let him in?

OLIVE

I guess you'll have to.

> (SALLY *goes to the front door, and admits* BILL PAGE. *He is about thirty-two, adult, quiet and attractive. He wears a Sergeant's stripes, and carries an evening paper and a tiny week-end toilet-case.*)

BILL

Miss Sally Middleton?

SALLY

Yes, won't you come in? Olive's here.

OLIVE

(*Coming into view—brightly*)

Bill—darling!

25

BILL

(*Coming in*)

Hello.
    (*They kiss.*)

OLIVE

Sally, this is Bill Page. Sally Middleton.

SALLY

How do you do?

BILL

How do you do?

SALLY

May I take your things? (*She takes his cap and bag and puts them on desk*) Let me give you a drink.

BILL

Thanks.

SALLY

Scotch?

BILL

Swell. (*Looking around*) This is very pleasant. I haven't been in an apartment like this for quite a time. It's two years since I was in New York.

OLIVE

How does it look to you?

BILL

Like every other place these days . . . a lot too full of soldiers. But it's still good. *You're* looking blooming.

26

OLIVE

(*Uncomfortably bright*)

Oh, yes, I'm fine.

BILL

I don't know whether you've made any plans for this week-end, but I've got a lot.

OLIVE

(*Miserably*)

You have?

BILL

I thought tonight, we'd just have a quiet dinner . . . not go anywhere afterwards . . . just concentrate on good food, good drink and good . . . (SALLY *hands him his glass*) Thank you so much. (*Then, turning back to* OLIVE) Then I thought tomorrow we might take in a theatre. There was a notice in the evening paper of a new musical that opened last night. I imagine it will be all sold out, but I thought that, being in the theatre, you might know some way of getting tickets. (*Pause*) How about it? Have you got any strings you can pull?

OLIVE

(*Nerving herself*)

Bill . . . I've got something to tell you. (SALLY *edges to the bedroom door*) Don't go, Sally.

SALLY

You left your glass in the bedroom.

OLIVE

I don't want another drink.

SALLY

I'll just get it. (*She goes into the bedroom, closing the door behind her.* BILL *notices this with slight surprise, as he turns back to* OLIVE. *In the bedroom,* SALLY *goes over to the window, looks out, draws the curtains and then sits, doing nothing, unwilling to return to the living room.*)

BILL

Well, what is it?

OLIVE

Bill, darling, I don't know how to tell you, but . . . I'm afraid our week-end's off.

BILL

How do you mean?

OLIVE

Darling, I can't come out with you. I . . . Listen, you didn't know I was married, did you?
(OLIVE *plays this scene with all the conviction possible. There must be no sense that she is lying, or doing it badly. Whether or not* BILL *is deceived is another question.*)

BILL

No—when?

OLIVE

About eighteen months ago. It didn't take. That's why I didn't tell you in Detroit.

BILL

Well?

28

OLIVE

Well, just this afternoon, he called me up. He's in the Navy. It's his last leave, and . . . he wanted to see me.

BILL

Yes?

OLIVE

I've got to have dinner with him.

BILL

Oh, that's tough for you. And for me.

OLIVE

I know.

BILL

Well, we'll meet later.

OLIVE

(*Quickly*)

Oh, darling, I can't. I . . .

BILL

What?

OLIVE

(*Very uncomfortable*)

Well, he . . . he *is* my husband. I mean, we're not divorced, or anything.

BILL

You mean—you're going back to him?

29

OLIVE

(*Not altogether liking this*)

Well, I . . . I don't know about permanently, but . . . it's his last leave, and . . .

BILL

(*Sparing her more*)

I see.

OLIVE

You're not mad at me?

BILL

No. But you can't expect me not to be a little disappointed. It's all right, though. These things happen. Not often, I guess, but . . .

OLIVE

I'll see you next time you get leave.

BILL

(*Smiling*)

Okay.

OLIVE

You do understand?

BILL

(*Smiling and patting her hand*)

Sure. Everything.

OLIVE

(*Not liking this, either*)

Bill, you're sweet. You always were. And, look, I've got to go. It's so late.

BILL

(*Rising*)

Right now?

OLIVE

I'm meeting Ned at eight.

BILL

What's his other name?

OLIVE

(*After a slight pause*)

Burling.

BILL

(*Looking at her*)

Mrs. Ned Burling! Who'd have thought it?

OLIVE

(*Very uncomfortable now*)

He's a Commander. I *must* go. (*Calls*) Sally! Sally!

BILL

Do you want me to take you anywhere?

OLIVE

(*Hurriedly*)

No . . . no . . . you stay here, and have your drink in peace. (SALLY *returns*) I've broken it to him, Sally, and he's been sweet.

SALLY

(*Smiling politely*)

Oh?

31

OLIVE

And now I've got to fly.

SALLY

It's started to rain.

OLIVE

Oh, hell, can you get a taxi anywhere around here?

SALLY

Sometimes on Third Avenue. But not when it's raining.

OLIVE

I'll find one. Good-bye, Bill, and do forgive me. I'll call you. Where are you staying?

BILL

I don't know yet. I went straight from the station to your hotel. I asked if they'd a room there, but they were all full up. So I just came on here.

OLIVE

(*Abashed*)

Oh, Bill . . . I should have gotten you a room. New York's so full, only . . .

BILL

Don't worry. I'll find something.

OLIVE

I'll call you too, Sally. Bless you, and . . . (*She breaks off, floundering, kisses her and goes to the door*) Good-bye, Bill.

BILL

Good-bye. Have fun.

OLIVE

(*Turning, reproachfully*)

Oh, Bill, that's not kind.

BILL

I'm sorry.

OLIVE

(*As before*)

No, it's not kind at all! (*She goes.*)

BILL

(*Turning to* SALLY, *with a slightly rueful grin*)

Well . . .

SALLY

(*Smiling*)

Well?

BILL

Give her a minute to get clear, and then I'll go along.

SALLY

There's no hurry.

BILL

Aren't you going out?

SALLY

No.

BILL

Well, all the same . . . I wonder if I might use your telephone.

33

SALLY

(*Going to the bedroom door*)

Yes, of course. It's in there.

BILL

Thank you so much.

(*He goes into the bedroom.* SALLY *closes the door on him,
to give him privacy, and then draws the curtains, lights
the lamps and settles down with the evening paper on the
couch. In the bedroom,* BILL *takes out a small notebook
from his pocket, looks up a number, dials it, sitting on the
bed.*)

BILL

Hello? Can I speak to Miss Westbury, please? Miss Joan
Westbury. Isn't that . . . (*Referring to his book again*) Butter-
field 8-1747? Don't Mr. and Mrs. Arthur Westbury live there?
Oh, I see. Can you tell me where they're living now? I see.
Thank you. (*Hangs up, gets notebook out again, and looks up
another number, dialing it*) Hello . . . Is Miss Van Huysen
there, please? Oh, are you expecting her in? Oh, I see. Well, will
you tell her, Monday, that Mr. Page called, Friday? Mr. Bill
Page, of Pittsburgh. No, no number. (*Hangs up again, and then
dials another number after a moment's reflection and search*)
Hello, is Mr. Frank Archer there? Frank? This is Bill Page.
Yes. Oh, I'm in town for the week-end. Say, you don't happen
to know Joan's number, do you? Joan Westbury. I called her old
number, but . . . no kidding? I hadn't heard. How does she
look in her uniform? Say, whatever happened to Alice . . . what
was her other name? That's right . . . Alice Hopewell. She *is*?
When did she *get* married? What—Phyllis, too? Well, that's
about all the old gang, isn't it? Frank, could *we* have some dinner
tonight? Oh, you are? That's all right. It was just that I got stood
up, that's all. Oh, I don't know. I'll probably go to the Stage

Door Canteen, or something. I'm not stopping *anywhere* at the moment. I'll call *you*. Sure. Good-bye. (*Hangs up again. Looks in book again, thumbing leaves . . . is about to dial another number, then mutters, "Oh, the hell with it. She's probably dead." Rises, looks out of window, says, "Oh, damn the rain!" and returns to the other room.*)

SALLY

(*Looking up with a polite smile*)

Did you get your number?

BILL

Yes, thanks. Well . . .

SALLY

Won't you have another drink?

BILL

You're sure you're in no hurry?

SALLY

None at all.

BILL

Well, then, thanks. I'd like to.

SALLY

Help yourself, won't you?

BILL

(*Going to drink-table*)

Will *you*?

35

SALLY

I don't think so, thanks. (*She watches him commiseratingly, but unable to think of anything to talk about.*)

BILL

(*Making conversation*)

Are you and Olive old friends?

SALLY

We are, rather. She was in the first play I was ever in.

BILL

Oh. I ought to know, of course, but I haven't been around. Are you a well-known actress?

SALLY

(*Laughing*)

Me? I've never been in anything but flops. My longest run was three weeks.

BILL

You're not in anything now?

SALLY

No, nor likely to be, for months.

BILL

(*Coming back with his drink*)

What do actresses do between jobs?

SALLY

Well, *I* just sit and think about how I'm going to act all the parts I'll never get a chance to act. Like Juliet, or Nina in *The Sea Gull*. That's a Russian play.

BILL

I know.

SALLY

Oh, I'm sorry. I didn't mean to be patronizing. Only not a lot of people do know, and I didn't know if you knew anything about the theatre. *I* don't know anything about real life.

BILL
(*Amused*)

Real life?

SALLY

I always think of it like that. I mean, all of us . . . actors, and authors, too . . . we aren't really living in the real world at all. We're giving our whole lives to . . . make-believe.

BILL
(*Sitting*)

Why do you do it, then?

SALLY

I guess because I'm made that way. And in the hope of . . .

BILL

Of some day seeing your name in lights?

SALLY

Oh, I hope it isn't that. Of course, it's part of it. It would be silly to pretend it wasn't. But the hope . . . of one day being able to express . . . well, that thing one feels one's got to express . . .

BILL

"That one Talent which is death to hide?"

SALLY

(*Struck*)

Oh . . . what's that?

BILL

Milton. The sonnet on his blindness.

SALLY

Oh . . . it's lovely. Say it again. Say it all.

BILL

I don't think I can remember it all. It's years since I've looked at it. But . . . (*Quietly*)

> "*When I consider how my light is spent*
> *Ere half my days in this dark world and wide,*
> *And that one Talent which is death to hide,*
> *Lodged with me useless . . .*"

I don't remember any more.

SALLY

(*Savoring it*)

Oh . . . yes.

BILL

Well, that's wonderful . . . if you *have* the talent.

SALLY

Have *you?* I mean . . . do you do anything creative?

BILL

No, I'm afraid the only talent *I've* ever had is a talent for appreciation.

SALLY

What *did* you do before the war?

BILL

I didn't do anything at all till I was twenty-five, except have a very good time.

SALLY

Were you a . . . playboy?

BILL

Well, that's not a thing one would ever think of oneself as being . . . but, I suppose—by present-day standards, anyway—that's what I was. My family had a lot of money . . . and I went to Princeton, and Europe and . . . appreciated things. Very much indeed.

SALLY

And then?

BILL

Well, then things went wrong with the family, and the business went smash, and I had to come back and buckle down to . . . "real life."

39

SALLY

Was that awful for you?

BILL

A little. I told myself it was good for me. I guess maybe it was.

SALLY

And then the Army?

BILL

Yes.

SALLY

And . . . afterwards?

BILL

I haven't any plans for afterwards. I just hope there'll still be things left to appreciate.

SALLY

There'll always be. So long as there are people. Free people. That's what it's all about, isn't it? The war, I mean?

BILL

You mustn't ask a soldier what the war's about.

SALLY

(*After a pause, tasting the phrase again*)

"That one Talent which is death to hide . . ."

BILL

(*Smiling at her*)

That sums you up, does it?

40

SALLY

Oh, no. Milton could say that. I'm not that conceited. But it's what it *feels* like, when you're out of work, or doing something second-rate. It's like having something *entrusted* to you . . . for the benefit of others . . . that you're wasting. (*Breaking off*) Oh, no . . . that sounds awful! Phony and arty, like Madame Pushkin.

BILL

Who's she?

SALLY

Madame Pushkin? Oh, she's an imaginary character that Olive and I invented. An old Russian actress who runs a school where she teaches the Pushkin method. Her husband, Dr. Pushkin, is a very great director, and every morning he chases her around the bedroom for one hour in her nightgown to "giff her de free body." Didn't Olive ever tell you about her?

BILL

Olive and I have never talked like this.

SALLY

(*Abashed*)

I'm sorry.

BILL

What for?

SALLY

Going on about myself.

BILL

I've liked it. And *I've* gone about myself, too . . . which is something I haven't done for years. Will you have dinner with me?

SALLY

(*After a second*)

Oh . . . no, thanks.

BILL

Why not?

SALLY

You don't have to ask me.

BILL

I know I don't. But will you?

SALLY

Well . . . we go Dutch.

BILL

No, I asked you.

SALLY

Only because Olive let you down.

BILL

Only because if she hadn't, I wouldn't have had the chance.

SALLY

(*Embarrassed by the compliment*)

Well, thank you very much, then.

BILL

Where shall we go?

42

SALLY

Wherever you say.

BILL

What's the place next door like?

SALLY

(*After a half-second's pause, with an echo in her ears*)
Very expensive.

BILL

But good?

SALLY

Yes, but . . .

BILL

Let's go there. (*He notices a hesitation about her*) Have you anything against it?

SALLY

N-no . . . But it's . . . *very* expensive.

BILL

All the same. Besides, it's raining quite hard now, so *let's* go next door. There was a restaurant of the same name in Paris that I used to go to quite a lot, once upon a time. Did you know Paris?

SALLY

No. I never went to Europe. I was only eighteen when the war broke out.

BILL

My God. That hurts.

43

SALLY

What?

BILL

That that's possible, already. (*He looks at her.*)

SALLY

(*After an embarrassed pause*)

I'll just get my coat. (*She starts into the bedroom.* BILL *stands looking after her.*)

CURTAIN

ACT ONE

Scene II

Scene: *The same. About 10:30 the same night.*
The stage is as we left it. Then the sound of a key is heard in the
front door. BILL *and* SALLY *come in.*

BILL

What a night! (*Closes the door behind him*) Did you get wet?

SALLY

Running from next door? No. Come in and sit down, won't
you?

> (BILL *shakes out his cap, and puts it down. He helps*
> SALLY *off with her coat. She switches on the lamps.*)

SALLY

Would you like a drink?

BILL

Not after all that brandy. I must have had five, waiting for the
rain to stop.

SALLY

(*After a moment's pause, going to the radio*)

Would you like the news?

BILL

I don't think so. Unless *you* would.

45

SALLY

I don't think . . . really. (*She starts to wander purposelessly*)
Have a candy? (*Offers box.*)

BILL

No, thanks. You don't have to entertain me, you know. Relax.
What are you fussing about?

SALLY

Was I fussing? I didn't mean to. (*Pause*) That was a lovely
dinner. Thank you.

BILL

You were right. It's a good place.

SALLY

It was better even than usual tonight. That was your remembering the proprietor from Paris. And he you. You must have
gone there a lot.

BILL

I did. I used to go with . . . a girl I used to go with. Almost
every evening, at one time, for weeks on end.

SALLY

Was it a famous place?

BILL

No, just tiny. But we used to think of it as "our" place. We
were very young.

SALLY

Were you in love with her?

BILL

I used to think I was.

46

SALLY

What happened to her?

BILL

She got married. Women do, you know.

SALLY

Yes. This isn't being a very amusing evening for you. Going to that restaurant . . . sort of upset you, didn't it?

BILL

Did that show?

SALLY

I *thought* . . .

BILL

I'm sorry. But "upset" is too strong a word. It was just . . . seeing it all done up exactly like the place in Paris, the same pictures on the walls, the same lamps on the tables, the same tablecloths . . . Well, it brought things back.

SALLY

The girl, you mean? Was she a French girl?

BILL

No, she was an American. I wasn't having an affair with Mimi, the little Midinette. But I didn't only mean the girl. I meant everything. Those were happy years. I was very happy then.

SALLY

And you're not now?

47

BILL

Is anyone?

SALLY

It's awful, but *I* am. Quite often.

BILL

It's not at all awful. It's wonderful. But I'm afraid I infected you at dinner. You were a bit low, too, I thought.

SALLY

(*Moving away*)

Well, strangely, that place has memories for *me*, too. More recent ones than yours, but . . .

BILL

Why didn't you tell me?

SALLY

(*Vaguely*)

Oh . . .

BILL

I'm afraid it wasn't a very good choice, for either of us.

SALLY

I *am* sorry. You're having a miserable time.

BILL

No, I'm having a grand time. (*Yawns*) Oh, I'm sorry.

SALLY

You see!

BILL

That wasn't misery . . . or boredom. It was too much dinner, and not enough sleep.

SALLY

Don't you get enough?

BILL

I haven't had enough for months. Tomorrow morning, I shall stay in bed till lunchtime. Sunday, I probably shan't get up at all . . . till it's time to go back.

SALLY

Is that how you want to spend your leave?

BILL

Well, there are worse ways.

SALLY

But it wasn't what you'd planned.

BILL

(*Putting out his cigarette*)

No! (*Then, after a second*) Did you know Olive was going to tell me all that story?

SALLY

(*Startled*)

What do you mean?

BILL

You don't think I believed it, do you? You didn't think I *would* believe it? (SALLY *stares at him*) Olive's far too . . . well, too frank and free a person, not to have mentioned a husband if she had one.

49

SALLY

But you haven't seen each other.

BILL

We saw each other in Detroit, six weeks ago.

SALLY

Yes, but then you . . .

BILL

What?

SALLY

(*Unable to go on, without giving away too much*)

Nothing.

BILL

Oh, she told you about it, did she? I guess girls always do.

SALLY

(*After just too long a pause*)

I don't know what you're talking about.

BILL

(*Smiling*)

Okay.

SALLY

(*Rising*)

Are you in love with Olive?

BILL

Is that your favorite question?

50

SALLY

(*Blushing and subsiding*)

I'm sorry.

BILL

I'm not in the least in love with her. So don't worry. I guess I'm a little sore at her for letting me down. But I'll get over that, by tomorrow.

SALLY

(*Slightly shocked*)

As quickly as that?

BILL

Oh, I think so. (*He yawns again*) Oh, I am sorry. I should be going.

SALLY

(*Rising*)

Well, if you're sleepy. Has the rain stopped?

BILL

I don't know. (*Goes to window and looks out*) No, I think it's worse.

SALLY

(*Following him to window*)

You can't go out in that.

BILL

If it doesn't let up soon, I'll have to.

SALLY

Well, don't go yet. It's sure to stop.

51

BILL

(*Returning to the couch*)

Tell me some more about Madame Pushkin.

SALLY

(*Laughing*)

Oh, it's silly.

BILL

No, I like the sound of her. What is the Pushkin Method?

SALLY

Well, to begin with, she believes that you must never play a part the way that it's written. That's too easy. (*Assuming a mock-Russian accent and personality*) Alvays you must look for de *odder* side of a character. Ven I play Lady Macbess, I concentrate on her . . . her *child-like* qvalities. Ven ve com to de scene from de sleep-valkings, *I* skip! (*And does so.*)

BILL

(*Laughing*)

You're a fool!

SALLY

(*Laughing, too*)

I know. There's heaps more. Her parents were on the stage, too, you know. She was conceived during an intermission of *The Cherry Orchard*.

BILL

Are you making all this up as you go along?

SALLY

Certainly. Olive and I do it for hours on end. We call it "How to be ham though high-brow." Olive . . . (*She stops a little self-consciously on the mention of* OLIVE's *name.*)

BILL

Look, you needn't get self-conscious about mentioning Olive's name to me. She hasn't broken my heart.

SALLY

Has anyone, ever? Did the girl in Paris?

BILL

At it again?

SALLY

Oh, dear, it's an obsession.

BILL

Why's it an obsession?

SALLY

I don't know. Because I'm a fool, I guess. I always think that everyone ought to be in love with *someone*.

BILL

Are *you*?

SALLY

I . . . I think I am.

BILL

Not sure? Have you been in love often?

53

SALLY

(*Seriously, considering it*)

No . . . not often.

BILL

(*Kidding her a little*)

I suppose actresses need to fall in love a lot . . . to be good actresses?

SALLY

(*Becoming Madame Pushkin instantly*)

Oh, *yes*, Meester Payche! Alvays ven I play a rôle I must be in lof. Sometimes I valk de streets for hours, to find someone to fall in lof viz! (*Telephone rings. She continues in the accent*) De telephone. Excuse please. I go. (*She goes into the bedroom, and turns on the light, answering the telephone very gaily, in Pushkin accents.* BILL *sits alone, amused, for a moment, then returns to the window, looks out again, then throws himself on the divan, below it, playing with the radio. He turns it on very softly to some gentle instrumental music, lights a cigarette, and stretches out full length on his back, listening to it.*)

SALLY

(*On the telephone*)

Hillo . . . (*Then, remembering, in her own voice*) I mean— hello. (*Then, recognizing* OLIVE'S *voice, she resumes the accent*) Is Madame Pushkin speakink, Miss Lashbrooke. (*Then, back to her own voice again*) I was just telling about her . . . To Bill . . . Yes, he's still here . . . No, we went out to dinner. . . . No, I've had a very *nice* evening. He wasn't a bit miserable. Where are you? . . . Well, it was a good thing you didn't, be- cause that *was* where we went. . . . Oh, we had the most won- derful Vichysoisse, and duck with oranges, salad with a lot of

garlic. . . . What? Yes, I guess we do . . . and Crêpes Suzettes
. . . Olive, you don't *mind* our having gone to dinner, do you?
It was just that he asked me, and he hadn't any other place to go
. . . No, I don't think he has. I don't think he's tried. . . . Well,
it's raining. Hard . . . Are *you* having fun? What did *you* have
to eat? . . . Oh, lovely. Yes, of course he's all right. Why not?
. . . Well, I won't tell him if you don't want me to. Good-bye,
Olive. (*She hangs up, a little bothered and puzzled. Then she re-
turns to the other room, where she stops at the sight of* BILL, *who
has fallen asleep, with the cigarette burning between his fingers.
She takes it gently from his hand, and he wakes.*)

BILL

(*Sitting up*)

What . . .? Oh, I'm sorry. I've been asleep.

SALLY

I'm sorry I woke you, but you might have set yourself on fire.
(*She gives him the cigarette back.*)

BILL

(*Rising*)

I might have set the place on fire. I'd better get along and look
for a hotel room.

SALLY

Yes, you'll have awful trouble, finding one. The hotels are all
full up.

BILL

Are they?

SALLY

Ol . . . (*She checks herself*) The friend who just called up
said they were.

BILL

(*Registering her change of phrase*)

Well, I'll dig up something. This is liable to keep up all night. So . . . (*He crosses to* SALLY, *extending his hand.*)

SALLY

(*As they shake hands, with a sudden thought*)

Would you want to stay here? That's a day-bed. It's quite comfortable.

BILL

I know it is. But . . . I don't think I should do that.

SALLY

I can give you a toothbrush.

BILL

I've got that with me.

SALLY

It seems silly to go out in all that rain. You'll get so wet looking for a taxi. You haven't any change of clothes. You're tired. I'll give you breakfast in the morning.

BILL

Oh, you needn't do that.

SALLY

I'd like to.

BILL

Well, it's very good of you . . .

56

SALLY

Then you will?

BILL

Yes, thank you. (*Yawns again*) Oh . . .

SALLY

(*Commiseratingly*)

Ah, look at you! Why don't you go to bed, right away? It's all made up. I've only got to take the cover off.

BILL

Let me help you.

SALLY

Oh, thank you. (*She takes the cushions from the day-bed, while* BILL *strips off the cover.*)

SALLY

(*After a moment*)

Would you like some pajamas?

BILL

I couldn't wear your pajamas.

SALLY

They aren't mine. They're men's pajamas. My . . . brother stays here sometimes.

BILL

Oh . . . well, then, thank you very much. That would be a luxury.

SALLY

I'll get them for you. (*She goes to the bedroom, taking her coat with her, and gets a pair of men's pajamas and bedroom slippers from a drawer. Meanwhile,* BILL *takes off his coat, hanging it over the back of a chair in the living room.* SALLY *returns.*)

SALLY

(*Handing him the pajamas*)

Here . . .

BILL

(*After the tiniest pause—taking them*)

Thanks. These are very resplendent.

SALLY

I brought you some slippers, too.

BILL

All the comforts of home. (*There is a tiny moment of embarrassment. Then he slumps onto the bed*) Gee, I'm tired. (*He starts to unlace his shoes.*)

SALLY

I'll just empty the ashtrays. (*She starts emptying them into the largest, while he continues to unlace his shoes. The radio starts playing the Londonderry Air, and she pauses, raising her head to listen to it.*)

BILL

(*Noticing*)

What is it?

(*She crosses to the radio, and turns it louder, to hear better. She smiles.*)

SALLY

That's my lucky tune.

BILL

The Londonderry Air?

SALLY

It's silly, but whenever I hear that, nice things always seem to happen to me. (*Collecting herself*) I'll just take these out. The bathroom's through there. (*She goes into the kitchen.* BILL *takes his toilet case and the pajamas and goes into the bathroom. In the kitchen,* SALLY *empties the ashtrays and washes them. Then she gets a tray with a Thermos set from the shelves, and fills the jug with ice-water from the icebox, taking the tray into the living room and setting it on the desk. She clears the drink-table of its tray, which she takes to the kitchen. Back in the living room again, she tidies the room, turning down the day-bed, and arranging the ottoman footrest of the armchair as a night-table, with the Thermos tray, cigarettes, matches, and ashtray, beside the bed. Throughout this business, the radio continues. Then she goes into the bedroom.*)

SALLY

(*Calling to the closed bathroom door*)

Have you everything you want?

BILL

(*Putting his head around the door, toothbrush in hand*)

Did you call?

SALLY

I said, have you everything you want?

59

BILL

Oh, sure, thanks. Everything.

> (*She smiles at him, and he shuts the door again. She strips the cover from her own bed, folds it and lays it on top of the chest of drawers. Then she goes back to the living room, switching off lights.* BILL *returns in pajamas, carrying his folded clothes. He looks around.*)

BILL

> (*Indicating a chair*)

This all right?

SALLY

Sure.

> (*He lays his clothes neatly across the chair.*)

BILL

> (*Coming to the bed*)

You don't know how good that looks. (*Sits on it*) And feels. (*He kicks off the slippers, and gets into bed*) And is. (*He sits up, smiling.*)

SALLY

What are you smiling at?

BILL

I was just remembering a novel I once read about life in 1910 . . . where the heroine was compromised because she was seen coming out a man's apartment, after dark.

SALLY

I guess things *have* changed.

BILL

You're not kidding.

SALLY

(*Dubiously*)

Although I don't know that my mother would . . . *quite* understand this. It's silly, because it couldn't be more sensible. But there are a lot of people still who wouldn't believe in it.

BILL

Well, don't tell 'em.

SALLY

I don't intend to. (*Pause*) Well . . . good night.

BILL

Good night, Sally.
　　(*He switches out the bed light.*)

SALLY

Good night, Cousin Bill.

BILL

Huh?

SALLY

Nothing. Oh, I left the kitchen light on. (*She goes back to the kitchen, talking from there, over her shoulder*) I'll just leave a note for Verona, to tell her not to disturb you. *If* she comes. (*She starts to scribble a note on a pad hanging on a nail*) Verona's the colored maid. I don't expect she'll show up, but I'll be on the safe side. (*She finishes the note, tears off the sheet and places it prominently. Then she switches off the kitchen light. The only remaining light is now in the bedroom. She returns to the dark living room.*)

SALLY

Are you all right?

(There is no answer. BILL *is asleep.* SALLY *tiptoes on into the bedroom, closing the door behind her. She sits on the bed, takes off her shoes, and is starting on her stockings as*

THE CURTAIN FALLS

Act Two

ACT TWO

Scene I

Scene: *The same. Around noon, the next day.*

When the curtain rises, BILL *is in the kitchen, squeezing orange juice at the sink. A coffee percolator is bubbling on the stove. A tray is set with cup and saucer and cream pitcher. The day-bed in the living room has been made, and in the bedroom* SALLY'S *bed has also been made, and the room tidied.*

After a moment, SALLY *lets herself in at the front door. She is in outdoor things, and carries some marketing bags, and a manuscript. Her manner is gay, and ever so slightly "high."* BILL *hears the door, and comes into the living room.*

BILL

Good morning.

SALLY

(*Dumping her packages on the couch*)

Good morning.

BILL

(*Smiling*)

How are you this morning?

SALLY

I'm fine. (*She looks around*) Is Verona here?

BILL

I haven't seen her.

SALLY

Did *you* make your bed?

BILL

Sure.

SALLY

You shouldn't have.

BILL

Why not?

SALLY

Because . . . it's not a man's thing to do.

BILL

You'd be surprised what a lot of men are doing it, nowadays.

SALLY

Yes, but this is your vacation. Have you had breakfast?

BILL

I've just put on some coffee, as you said in your note I might.

SALLY

I was *afraid* Verona wasn't going to show up. I meant to get your breakfast myself, but I had to go out.

BILL

Did *you* have breakfast?

SALLY

No. I had a cocktail.

66

BILL

A what?

SALLY

A cocktail.

BILL

When?

SALLY

Oh, about half an hour ago. It's made me a little heady.

BILL

Didn't you have any breakfast *before* the cocktail?

SALLY

No, there wasn't time. I thought if you were still here, and hadn't a date, we might have lunch. I did some marketing.

BILL

You seem to have done a lot.

SALLY

I can never resist a delicatessen. I hate eating alone, except things you can sort of cuddle up on the couch with . . . like potato salad. (*She pats the package, indicating it.*)

BILL

I should never have thought of cuddling up with potato salad.

SALLY

I'd better take these in the kitchen. (*She starts to do so, talking as she goes*) I wish I'd started housekeeping before rationing. It

67

must have been so easy, then. I always do everything too late. (*She returns to the living room*) It's the loveliest spring morning out. The weather's changed at last. In more ways than one, I think.

BILL

What do you mean by that?

SALLY

I think *my* weather's changed, too. I've got a job.

BILL

You have?

SALLY

That's what I went out about. That's what I had the cocktail about, too. They called me at half-past nine. I didn't disturb you, did I? I tried not to.

BILL

I didn't know a thing till half-past eleven.

SALLY

I was afraid the telephone might have woken you. (*Correcting herself*) Wakened you. But you were still sleeping when I left.

BILL

Not snoring, I hope?

SALLY

No, you were very peaceful. (*Turning to him with her characteristic sudden directness*) Don't you think there's something rather . . . frightening about people asleep? They look so unlike themselves, and sort of . . . vulnerable. I always feel one oughtn't to look.

68

BILL

When you have to sleep with fifty other men every night, you get over feeling like that.

SALLY

Do you hate it all?

BILL

(*Briefly*)

No.

SALLY

Like it?

BILL

That would be going a little far. I don't think you're expected to *like* it.

SALLY

A job to be done?

BILL

You do like to talk about things, don't you?

SALLY

Yes, it's my besetting sin. I always hope if I talk about things, it will help me know what I feel about them. But it never does. It only muddles me more. (*Looking at him*) You're depressed this morning.

BILL

No, I just haven't had my coffee yet. It should be ready by now. You'd better have some, too.

SALLY

I'm not depressed.

BILL

(*With meaning*)

No, I know . . .

SALLY

You think I'm tight.

BILL

(*Unconvincingly*)

No, I don't.

SALLY

I am. A little. And I'm happy, too.

BILL

(*As they go into kitchen*)

Tell me about the job.

SALLY

Oh, it's a lovely job. Only . . . may I tell you when we sit down? I hate telling a story in bits . . . if it's a good story.

BILL

All right. (*He gets another cup and saucer from the shelves, and puts it on the tray.* SALLY *starts putting her packages in the icebox*) By the way, your telephone rang while you were out. It rang twice.

SALLY

Oh, who was it?

BILL

I don't know.

SALLY

Didn't you answer?

70

BILL

No.

SALLY

Why not?

BILL

I didn't think it would sound very well to have a man's voice answering your telephone.

SALLY

I wouldn't have thought of that.

BILL

Suppose it had been your Aunt Minnie from Duluth? Or . . . your brother, for that matter?

SALLY

My . . .?

BILL

(*Quickly*)

Whose very handsome pajamas I wore last night.

SALLY

Oh . . . yes. (*He takes the tray and goes into the living room.* SALLY *follows with the percolator*) You mean you just let it ring? I don't think I could do that, even in someone else's house. It always sounds to me as if it was going crazy when I don't answer. Besides, it might be something lovely.

BILL

(*Setting the tray down and sitting down to it with her*)

For instance?

71

SALLY

(*Pouring coffee*)

Well . . . a long-lost uncle with a lot of money, or a lovely party, or a job.

BILL

How often has it been one of those?

SALLY

It was a job this morning.

BILL

Yes, you win on that. (*Takes his cup*) Now do you feel settled enough to tell about it?

SALLY

(*Taking hers*)

Yes, I think so. Well, as I say, it's really a lovely job. It's a play that's in rehearsal already. I knew about it from a friend of mine who was going to be in it. Well, yesterday was the fifth day. Oh, I don't guess you know about that. You can fire actors up to the fifth day, if they're no good.

BILL

No, I didn't know. What happens *after* the fifth day?

SALLY

You have to keep them, or pay them two weeks' salary. It's a rule of Equity. Well, it seems they fired her yesterday.

BILL

Your friend?

72

SALLY

Yes. I feel sort of badly about that . . . getting her part, I mean . . . though, actually, she couldn't have been in it very long, if it had run, because she's going to have a baby, only she didn't tell them that. And I don't think it was quite honorable. I mean, it may be an act of God, but not if it's already started, I should think.

BILL

(*Bewildered*)

What *are* you talking about? What may be an act of God?

SALLY

Having a baby. It is, in the theatre.

BILL

I never knew the theatre was that different. I see now what you mean about real life! Well, go on . . . They fired her, and sent for you?

SALLY

Yes. I'm starting rehearsals Monday. The author took me next door for a cocktail, and I didn't like to tell him I hadn't had any breakfast. It sounded too pathetic. And then he told me something really thrilling.

BILL

What was that?

SALLY

Well, I'm not supposed to tell. But . . . well, you don't know anyone in the theatre, do you?

BILL

Only Olive.

SALLY

Well, I don't guess you'll be seeing her.

BILL

I guess not.

SALLY

I think I can tell you. You see, the leading man isn't very good, but he was all they could get, because of the draft.

BILL

You mean——he's 4-F?

SALLY

I guess so. Anyway, his acting's 4-F. Well, now, with Olive's tour closing, there's a chance they might get Henry Atherton. And that'd be wonderful. I've always had the most terrific crush on him.

BILL

(*Surprised*)

That weazened, whimsy little man with dyed gold hair?

SALLY

Oh, he's sweet. And it's not dyed. Is it?

BILL

Olive said it was. And she said he used to make passes at all the kids in the company.

SALLY

Yes, she told me. But he's a great star, and it would be a big chance for me. I told you last night that was my lucky tune.

BILL

What kind of a part have you got in this play?

SALLY

Oh, a lovely part. I have to go mad in one act. Do you know anything about insanity?

BILL

Not a thing. Why?

SALLY

I thought you might give me some pointers. Although, as a matter of fact, I know just how I want to do it, if I can.

BILL

How is that?

SALLY

I want to play it very quietly, and as if I thought I were quite sane, myself. I mean, I don't imagine mad people ever *think* they're mad. They probably think everyone else is.

BILL

(*In Pushkin accents*)

You are qvite right. Dat is how I teach my vife, Madame Pushkin, to play Ophelia.

SALLY

I don't go *very* mad. I mean, not straws and things.

BILL

I'm glad of that. I don't like plays where people go *very* mad.

SALLY

Nor do I. Though they're fun to do. What other kinds of plays don't you like?

BILL

Plays about men who are paralyzed from the waist down. Plays where a lot of people all get caught together in a catastrophe —a flood, or an earthquake, or an air raid—and all face death in a lump. There's always a prostitute in those plays, have you noticed? Usually a clergyman, too. That's what's called "taking a cross-section of humanity." I don't like plays about prostitutes.

SALLY

They're lovely to act. Olive's played lots. I haven't been one since I was in high school. And then they called it a courtesan.

BILL

(Laughing)

I bet you were immense. (*He rises to get cigarettes from the pocket of his coat which is hanging over a chair.* SALLY *rises, too, taking the percolator back to the kitchen.*)

BILL

Well, things *are* looking up for you. I guess you're right, and the weather *has* changed. The rain is over, the winter is past, and the voice of the turtle is heard in our land.

SALLY

(Arrested in the doorway)

What did you say?

BILL

I was quoting from the Bible.

SALLY

Oh. (*She comes back for the tray, and then stops again, worriedly*) But turtles don't *have* voices . . . do they?

BILL

Turtle *dove*.

SALLY

Oh. (*As she goes back to the kitchen with the tray*) I never could understand the Bible. I don't see why they give it to children to read. (*She returns to the living room.*)

BILL

You know, we ought to do something to celebrate this job of yours. Will you have dinner with me?

SALLY

You took me to dinner last night.

BILL

So what?

SALLY

So you shouldn't do it again.

BILL

But I want to do it again. Very much. And what do you say we go to a theatre? That new musical. Do you like musicals?

SALLY

I adore them. If they're good.

BILL

Well, this is supposed to be very good.

SALLY

Yes, it is. I've heard some of the songs.

BILL

Well, let's go, then.

SALLY

We'd never get seats.

BILL

Not even through a broker?

SALLY

I don't think so. After those notices . . . and the first Saturday.

BILL

I wondered whether Olive mightn't have some pull. I started to ask her yesterday.

SALLY

I know. But I don't think she has. And I wouldn't want to ask her now, anyway.

BILL

Why not?

SALLY

Well, you're *her* friend, and Olive's rather hot against that kind of thing. Beau-snatching. I don't know that I really ought to come at all.

BILL

Now you listen to me. In the first place, you haven't snatched me. Any snatching that's been going on, *I*'ve been doing. And in the second, I'm not her beau . . . any more. She gave me the

78

good, old-fashioned gate last night, even though I did suspect she was trying to leave it on the latch. The point is, we're going to that musical. How *does* one get tickets for a show like that, at the last moment? People do.

SALLY

Well, there are things called house seats.

BILL

What are they?

SALLY

They're tickets that the management keeps up its sleeve for friends, and influential people.

BILL

Who is the management?

SALLY

Kenneth Bartlett's putting it on.

BILL

Do you know him?

SALLY

(*Remotely*)

Yes, I . . . know him.

BILL

Well, then call him up. Tell him a friend of yours . . . a service man . . . is in town . . . you can say it's his last furlough . . .

SALLY

(*Faintly alarmed*)

Is it?

79

BILL

No, but it makes a better story. And can he please buy two of the house seats for tonight? (SALLY *sits dumbly*) What's the matter?

SALLY

I can't ask him.

BILL

Don't you know him well enough?

SALLY

It isn't that.

BILL

What then?

SALLY

It's just that . . . I can't. There are reasons. Really, there are. I can't.

BILL

Well, then, I'll go foraging this afternoon when I look for a hotel room, and you can stay here and study how to go slightly mad.

SALLY

I'm afraid you won't get anything.

BILL

Well, don't be so worried about it.

SALLY

But you wanted to see it. You're having an awful leave. You're not doing any of the things you planned to do.

BILL

I'm enjoying the things I'm doing, instead.

SALLY

(*Suddenly, as always*)

Do you believe in pride?

BILL

Now what do you mean by that?

SALLY

Suppose someone had . . . not treated you badly, it's not that . . . suppose you'd behaved badly to someone . . . do you think you ought to ask them for a favor?

BILL

I should hardly think so. What's this about? The theatre tickets?

SALLY

(*Quickly*)

No. Oh, no. Just general principles.

BILL

Have *you* behaved badly to someone?

SALLY

Well, not badly in the ordinary sense. But . . . well . . . What's the difference between true pride and false?

BILL

I really wouldn't know.

SALLY

I'm sure you oughtn't to.

BILL

Oughtn't to what?

SALLY

Ask the favor.

BILL

(*After a moment*)

Well, let's stop this abstract speculation and get lunch.

SALLY

(*Coming out of her reverie*)

Oh . . . yes. (*She rises.*)

BILL

Sally.

SALLY

What?

BILL

You're very sweet. (*She looks up at him with surprise. He takes her hands*) I haven't the faintest idea what goes on in that funny little head of yours, but you're very sweet. (*He leans forward and kisses her, gently. They hold the kiss for a moment, then he releases her.*)

SALLY

Oh . . . that was a surprise.

BILL

Do you mind?

82

SALLY

No, it was nice.

BILL

I thought so, too. Come and show me where things are. (*He goes into the kitchen. She follows him, more disturbed than ever*) What are we going to have? Not potato salad, I hope?

SALLY

(*Still in a slight trance*)

No, I thought maybe . . . scrambled eggs.

BILL

Good.

SALLY

(*Reaching down below stove*)

I'll get the frying pan.

BILL

Do you have a double boiler? I think they're better in a double boiler.

SALLY

(*Bringing one out, abstractedly*)

Are they? I've never used one.

BILL

Do you like them wet or dry?

SALLY

What?

BILL

Your eggs.

SALLY

Oh . . . wet, I think.

BILL

Good. So do I. And how about coming out of that trance?

SALLY

I'm sorry. (*Then, suddenly*) Will you excuse me a minute? (*She leaves quickly and goes to the bedroom, closing the door firmly behind her. She looks at the telephone hesitantly for a moment, then sits, grasps it with determination, and dials. Meanwhile* BILL *is collecting things for the meal in the kitchen—eggs, milk, pepper, salt, etc., filling the base of the double boiler and putting it on the stove. Into phone*) Hello? Is Mr. Bartlett there? Miss Middleton. Miss Sally Middleton. Thanks. (*She holds on nervously*) Hello . . . Ken? Yes. I'm fine. Ken, I wonder if I can ask you a favor? . . . Well, a friend of mine . . . a soldier . . . is in town on leave, and he wanted terribly to go to your show tonight. I wondered if you had any seats left he could buy . . . Well, two . . . yes, yes, I was going with him . . . You could? Oh, that's wonderful. It was the only thing he wanted to see and . . . it's terribly nice of you . . . Oh, are you going to be there? Good. Yes, yes, of course, we'd like to . . . Page. Sergeant Page . . . Oh, that's sweet of you. I do appreciate it . . . Ken, I read the notices. I'm so glad it's such a hit. Well, thank you again . . . so much. Good-bye, Ken. (*She hangs up with a little exhausted* "Phew" *from the strain, then returns to the kitchen.*)

BILL

(*Breaking eggs into a bowl*)

Now come and learn how to make scrambled eggs properly.

84

SALLY

All right.

BILL

First you break the eggs.

SALLY

Yes, I do know that.

BILL

Oh . . . do you have an egg-beater?

SALLY

(*Getting it*)

Yes. It's always scared me to death.

BILL

They're better if you beat them.

SALLY

(*As* BILL *breaks the last egg*)

Bill . . .

BILL

(*Pausing*)

What?

SALLY

It's all right about tonight. I've got the tickets.

BILL

You have? How?

85

SALLY

I called up Kenneth Bartlett. They're at the theatre, in your name. You're to pick them up by seven o'clock. He wants us to have a drink with him in the intermission.

BILL

Good. What's he like?

SALLY

He's nice. Very nice.

BILL

What made you suddenly change your mind?

SALLY

I don't know. Yes, I do.

BILL

What was it?

SALLY

Your kissing me.

BILL

I don't quite see the connection.

SALLY

I don't think I could explain.

BILL

May I kiss you again for getting them?

SALLY

If you want to.

86

BILL

I do. (*He kisses her again*) Thank you.

SALLY

(*Smiling*)

Thank *you.*

BILL

We're going to have a nice evening. Now then . . . (*He starts beating the eggs.*)

CURTAIN

ACT TWO

SCENE II

SCENE: *The same. Two* A.M.
When the curtain rises, the stage is in darkness. The radio is playing. The announcer's voice is heard.

ANNOUNCER

W.O.T.C. New York. Two A.M., Saturn Watch time. We bring you now an electrically transcribed program of the latest dance rhythms.

> (*Music starts. After it has been playing a moment the telephone begins to ring. After three or four rings, the front door opens.* BILL *and* SALLY *come in. She wears a dinner dress under a day coat.*)

SALLY

It is! I told you it was! (*She starts for the bedroom.*)

BILL

Wait a minute. You don't want to answer that.

SALLY

> (*Arrested*)

Why not?

BILL

Because you know perfectly well who it is.

SALLY

(*Whispering*)

Olive?

BILL

Sure. And I don't know what you're whispering for. She can't possibly hear you. (SALLY *stands irresolute, looking at him pleadingly. The bell continues*) Do you want to talk to her . . . now?

SALLY

Not really.

BILL

(*Takes her hand and pulls her toward sofa*)

Well, then this is your chance for a first lesson in self-control with the telephone. Sit down, and let it ring.

(SALLY *sits down. The telephone continues. It is obviously an effort to her to stay where she is.* BILL *switches on the lamps and stands watching her with amusement. Silence for a moment. Then she leaps up.*)

SALLY

It's no good. I can't stand it.

(*The telephone stops.*)

BILL

There. It's all over. It's stopped.

SALLY

I feel as if it had died. And I'd killed it. (*She now notices the radio*) Did you turn the radio on?

BILL

No.

SALLY

Then it must have *been* on. We must have left it on. (*She goes to radio and turns it off*) It must have been playing all evening . . . all by itself.

BILL

(*Amused*)

Does that bother you, too?

SALLY

Yes, it does. Sort of hurting its feelings . . . no one listening.

BILL

You're crazy.

SALLY

(*Taking off her coat*)

It's sort of spooky, too. The telephone and the radio, both going, and no one paying any attention. It's like . . . like a world where everyone's dead, and *they're* still going on.

BILL

(*Taking the coat from her*)

You have pretty fancies, don't you? I hate to spoil it, but if everyone *were* dead, there wouldn't be any telephone and radio to *go* on.

SALLY

Why not?

BILL

Because they don't work without human agency . . . yet.

90

SALLY

I don't think of things like that. Isn't it funny, to think that all those things, like electricity, were there all the time . . . just waiting to be discovered?

BILL

I bet they got awfully impatient. Thought Benjamin Franklin and Marconi were just *never* coming along.

SALLY

(*Looking worried*)

Oh . . .

BILL

Stop it.

SALLY

What?

BILL

Getting sorry for electricity.

SALLY

(*Laughing*)

Oh . . . I was, too. (*She rises*) Do you want a drink?

BILL

I could do with a nightcap. Are you going to have one?

SALLY

I think I'll have a glass of milk . . . if you don't mind.

BILL

Why should I mind?

91

SALLY

Men do . . . sometimes.

BILL

I wish you'd stop thinking that *I'm* "men." As a matter of fact, I'll have a glass of milk, too.

SALLY

(*As they go through to the kitchen*)

Good. Would you like some cookies? My mother made them. She sent them to me.

BILL

(*Taking the cookie jar*)

Where does your mother live?

SALLY

(*Getting the milk from the icebox*)

At home. Joplin, Missouri.

BILL

I've never been to Joplin.

SALLY

(*Pouring two glasses*)

Why should you?

BILL

Have you a large family?

SALLY

Um. Rather.

BILL

Are you fond of them?

92

SALLY

Yes, very. Only I can't stand them for more than two weeks at a time, any more. That's sad, don't you think?

BILL

I think it's natural.

SALLY

I hate myself for it. But it's no good, trying. That's another reason why I'm so happy about this job coming now. I was afraid I'd have to go back home for the summer.
(*They return to the living room, settling on the couch, with the milk and cookies.*)

SALLY

(*As they go*)

I guess a family's really only good when you're sick . . . once you're grown up. And I'm never sick. So . . . (*Sitting and taking up her milk*) I wonder if that *was* Olive on the telephone?

BILL

She's probably been calling ever since we left the theatre.

SALLY

It was too bad we had to run into her. We should have seen her in the intermission. Or afterwards. She'll think we were avoiding her.

BILL

Sure. That's why she's calling.

SALLY

But we weren't. We couldn't help it.

93

BILL

(*Eating, calmly*)

I know.

SALLY

Doesn't that worry you?

BILL

(*As before*)

Not a bit. I didn't think the guy looked so hot, did you? Of course, I may be prejudiced, but I don't think *I*'d have turned down *me* for him.

SALLY

I was a *little* disappointed.

BILL

(*After a pause, watching her*)

I liked your friend, Kenneth Bartlett.

SALLY

(*Eagerly*)

He *is* nice, isn't he?

BILL

I thought he was grand. He likes you, too.

SALLY

How do you know?

BILL

He said so. Told me what a grand kid you were, and a good little actress . . . and generally tops.

94

SALLY

(*Wondering a little*)

Did he? When?

BILL

In the men's room at the Plaza. That's where men always tell each other things like that.

SALLY

You didn't *mind* our going on with his party, did you?

BILL

No, it was a good party. I've had a grand evening. And a grand day. Except that I've not seen much of *you*.

SALLY

(*Laughing*)

You've seen me steadily for the last thirty hours!

BILL

I haven't. I slept ten of them, damn it. Spent three alone this afternoon getting a hotel room . . . sat beside you in a crowded theatre all evening, and shared you with a party of ten ever since. Will you spend tomorrow with me, to make up?

SALLY

I'd love to.

BILL

Good. (*There is a small pause. He rises, walking away and looking into his milk*) Did you notice the girl at the Persian Room that I went over to talk to?

SALLY

Yes.

95

BILL

Do you know who that was?

SALLY

No. Not . . .?

BILL

(*Nodding*)

That was the girl from Paris.

SALLY

It's been that kind of an evening! How . . . how long since you'd seen her?

BILL

Seven years.

SALLY

Not *since* Paris?

BILL

We said good-bye at the Gare du Nord, on May the second, 1936.

SALLY

Were you engaged, or anything?

BILL

We were engaged, and *every*thing. We were going to be married that summer. But that was the summer that things busted up for me. She couldn't see herself living in Pittsburgh, with no money.

96

SALLY

She married someone else, you said. Was that her husband with her tonight?

BILL

Yes. This *is* my evening for running into my successors, isn't it?

SALLY

What was he like?

BILL

Well, there again I guess I'm prejudiced.

SALLY

Was it *awful* . . . seeing her again?

BILL

No. Not after the first moment. And that was funny, because . . . last night at the restaurant it did get me down, remembering it all. And then the minute we'd said hello, the corner of my mouth suddenly stopped twitching, and I found myself looking at her and wondering what the hell it had all been about. I don't know *when* I stopped loving her—I just stopped thinking of her, I guess, and didn't realize I had . . . until tonight. Last night must have been just a . . . sort of reflex action.

SALLY

Haven't you been in love since?

BILL

(*Briefly*)

No. Nor wanted to. That was quite enough.

97

SALLY

You don't believe in being in love?

BILL

I don't believe in being unhappily in love, and I'm not taking chances.

SALLY

I know what you mean. Does it feel . . . good, to be over it?

BILL

Good, but a little shocking, if you've been cherishing the illusion that you weren't.

SALLY

Yes. (*Then looking away from him, after a pause*) I was in love with Kenneth Bartlett. At least, I thought I was.

BILL

(*Quietly*)

I know.

SALLY

How do you know?

BILL

(*Quickly*)

Oh, he didn't tell me. I guessed. (*Gently*) Did *you* find you were over it tonight?

SALLY

(*Nodding*)

I was dreading seeing him at the theatre. And then he came up to us, and it was all right. I just thought how nice he was.

98

BILL

That's wonderful. I wish *I'd* been able to think that . . . about *her*.

SALLY

I'm sorry you couldn't. It's a good feeling. But you're right. It *is* a little shocking.

BILL

I think it's only one's vanity that's shocked. One likes to think one's the kind that *doesn't* get over things.

SALLY

But you do think one *ought* to . . . get over them, I mean?

BILL

Good God, yes. (*He sits beside her on the couch.*)

SALLY

(*After a pause*)

It's funny our being in the same boat.

BILL

It's a good boat. (*Taking her hand*) Sally . . .

SALLY

What?

BILL

You don't think . . . *my* coming along had anything to do with helping to set you free, do you?

99

SALLY

I . . . don't know.

BILL

I'd like to think it did.

SALLY

I think it did.

BILL

I'm glad.

SALLY

So am I . . . Did . . . (*She stops*) No, I won't ask that.

BILL

Why not?

SALLY

No, I won't.

BILL

Were you going to ask whether *your* coming along helped to set *me* free?

SALLY

You don't have to answer that. And I *didn't* ask it.

BILL

If I say I think I was free already . . . let me say, too, that I think it was your coming along that helped me *know* I was, and that I'm very grateful.

SALLY

I'm glad.

100

BILL

So am I. (*He draws her to him and kisses her*) You're very sweet.

SALLY

You're very nice.

BILL

I couldn't have imagined . . . possibly . . . having so nice a time as this.

SALLY

Me, too. I've had such miserable week-ends here alone.
(*Silence for a moment. He continues to fondle her, his lips against her hair and cheek, moving toward her lips again. Again they kiss. Then, suddenly, she thrusts him aside, and rises abruptly and agitatedly.*)

BILL

What's the matter?

SALLY

We mustn't go on like this.

BILL

Why not?

SALLY

Because I've given it up!

BILL

What?

SALLY

That sort of thing.

BILL

For Lent?

SALLY

No . . . permanently.

BILL

(*Protesting, laughing*)

Oh, Sally . . . darling . . .

SALLY

I have. I'm sorry, but I have.

BILL

Why have you?

SALLY

I *can't* go on doing it with every man I meet.

BILL

(*Amused*)

Do you?

SALLY

I *did*. No, I didn't, *really*, but . . . I've got to draw the line somewhere.

BILL

So you draw it at me?

SALLY

There's nothing personal about it. I do *like* you, but . . . we mustn't go on like that.

102

BILL

I'm sorry. Do you want me to go?

SALLY

No, but, well, maybe you'd rather.

BILL

Because you won't let me make love to you?

SALLY

Yes.

BILL

Is this another of your theories about "men"?

SALLY

It's a true one. If you start something like that . . . well, you've no right to start it, if you don't mean to go through with it. And I *don't* mean to . . . and I *shouldn't* have started it. And you've every right to be mad at me.

BILL

I'm not mad at you.

SALLY

Aren't you?

BILL

No, I think you're absurd, but sweet.

SALLY

I'm terribly sorry.

BILL

It's all right . . . so long as you like me.

SALLY

I do.

BILL

And you'll see me tomorrow?

SALLY

If you still want to.

BILL

Sure, I want to. I want to see you *all* tomorrow.

SALLY

I thought you were going to sleep all day.

BILL

That was in another life. What shall we do?

SALLY

Do you want to come to breakfast?

BILL

Yes, please. What time?

SALLY

What time would you like it?

BILL

Any time. Nine o'clock?

SALLY

Certainly.

BILL

And then?

SALLY

Well, if it's fine, and it really looked tonight as if it might be
. . . we can . . . walk in the Park . . . go to the Zoo . . . take
a bus some place. Up to the Cloisters, maybe.

BILL

That sounds swell. Well, if we're breakfasting at nine . . .
(*He makes a move.*)

SALLY

We don't have to. Why don't you call me when you wake up?

BILL

I might not wake up. And I don't want to waste any of tomorrow with you. I'll leave a call for eight o'clock.

SALLY

Oh, but that's awful for you. Eight o'clock on Sunday morning when you're on leave.

BILL

I don't mind. Would *you* like to call me when *you* wake up?

SALLY

No, I don't mind waking at eight.

BILL

You won't have to. You can sleep till half-past.

SALLY

I don't see that *either* of us has to. Why don't you stay here again?

BILL

Do you mean that?

SALLY

If you weren't too uncomfortable.

BILL

What sort of places do you think I've *been* sleeping in this last year?

SALLY

Well, then, please do. Then you can sleep as late as you want in the morning, and we'll just do whatever we feel like. I like days like that.

BILL

So do I.

SALLY

(*Worried again*)

Of course, it does waste your hotel room.

BILL

And disappoints the Hotel Taft. But I think it can take that.

SALLY

Well, then, will you?

BILL

(*After a tiny pause*)

Sure. Thanks.

106

SALLY

Do you want to turn in now?

BILL

Well, it's almost three. I should think I might. (*Goes to divan, and strips cover*) This is where I came in!

SALLY

You haven't got your bag this time. You'll want a toothbrush. I'll get it for you.

BILL

Why don't you go ahead, and get yourself to bed first? You were up hours earlier than I was.

SALLY

I'm all right.

BILL

No, do. You don't have to play hostess to me tonight. (*He gives her her coat*) I'll tidy up, and empty the ashtrays . . . Go on.

SALLY

All right, then. I won't be long. (*She goes into the bedroom, taking her coat, strips her bed cover, and takes off her shoes.* BILL *performs the night ritual with the ashtrays, drinks the last of his milk, and takes the glasses, cookie jar and ashtrays into the kitchen. Meanwhile* SALLY *tries to get out of her dress, but the zipper catches. She tugs at it for quite a while, despairingly. Then she calls*) Bill! Bill! (*But* BILL *is in the kitchen and does not hear. She comes into the living room and calls again*) Bill! Where are you, Bill?

(BILL *emerges from the kitchen.*)

BILL

Were you calling?

SALLY

Yes, my zipper's stuck.

BILL

Oh. Let me see. (*He examines it.*)

SALLY

I've pulled and pulled. (*He fidgets with it*) It's never done this, before.

BILL

Yes, it's good and stuck. It's a good thing I'm here, or you'd have had to sleep in it. You still may, of course. Have you a pair of pliers?

SALLY

There are some tools in the kitchen in a box on the floor under the sink. (BILL *goes for them*) I don't really know what's there. I'm the kind who's no use with tools. Even keys won't work for me, and then someone else comes along, and it turns as easily as anything. (*She fidgets again with her zipper*) You know, this is one of my nightmares, having this happen to me in the theatre . . . during a quick change.

BILL

(*In kitchen*)

Here we are.

SALLY

(*Calling*)

Find it?

108

BILL

(*Returning*)

Found it. Now then, hold still, take a deep breath, and I'll try not to hurt. (*He applies the pliers, missing the first time*) Damn. That's better . . . now it's coming . . . there! (*The zipper unzips, and her dress falls to the floor, leaving her in her slip*) Oh, I'm sorry. I'm afraid that was rather overdoing it.

SALLY

(*Stooping and picking up her dress*)

Thank you so much.

BILL

(*Embarrassed*)

Girls who wear zippers shouldn't live alone. Modern proverb.

SALLY

Well . . . thank you. (*She is about to go. He catches her.*)

BILL

Sally . . . (*He kisses her, and she responds. As the kiss threatens to grow more passionate, she pulls herself away.*)

SALLY

(*Releasing herself, as he tries to hold her*)

Don't, Bill . . . please don't. (*He lets her go. She goes back to the bedroom, where she stands a moment, fighting tears. Then she hangs her dress in the closet, with her coat, and goes through to the bathroom.*)

    (*Bill stands looking after her. Then he shrugs, turns down the day-bed, removes his coat, sits and unlaces one*

shoe and takes it off. He is about to start the second shoe,
when he stops, looking first at his bed and then at the
bedroom door.)

BILL

(*To himself*)

No, this is all too god-damned silly! (*He puts his shoe on*
again, and also his coat. Then he goes to the desk, takes paper and
pencil and starts to write a note.)

(SALLY *comes back into the bedroom, wearing pajamas,*
and looking very small and young. Her mood is still mel-
ancholy, and she is near tears. She switches out the lights,
except for the bed lamp, and gets into bed.)

(*During the above* BILL *has finished his note. He lays it*
on the day-bed, switches off the lamps and takes his cap,
going to the door, as SALLY *calls:*)

SALLY

(*In a muffled voice*)

Bathroom's all clear. (*He hears her, and stands with his hand*
on the knob of the front door) Bill! I said the bathroom's all
clear. (*He goes over, cap in hand, and opens the bedroom door.*)

BILL

Sally, I'm not staying. (*He comes into the room.*)

SALLY

Why not?

BILL

Because it's silly.

SALLY

Why?

BILL

Well, because . . . as they'd say in one of those plays we both hate . . . because I'm a man, and you're a woman.

SALLY

(*After a tiny pause—gravely, but with quote marks*)

And I . . . rouse the beast in you?

BILL

Exactly . . . So . . . I'll see you tomorrow. (*He starts to go.*)

SALLY

Bill . . . there's a beast in me, too! (*He stands looking at her, and then comes slowly to the bed*) I'm sorry, Bill, for being such a fool.

BILL

(*Tenderly*)

Sally . . . (*He sits on the bed and takes her in his arms. She melts into them. In the kiss*) Oh, Sally, sweet . . .

SALLY

Oh, Bill . . . (*The telephone rings. She starts, disengages herself, stretching out her hand, automatically, to answer it.*)

BILL

(*Slapping her hand*)

Uh huh. No, no!

SALLY

(*Looking stricken*)

Oh . . . (*He draws her into his arms again. She remains pressed against him, her cheek against his, looking at the telephone with scared eyes. Whispering*) You shouldn't be here.

BILL

Ssh.

SALLY

She'll come around in the morning.

BILL

Let the morning look after itself. (*He kisses her again, and without breaking the embrace, switches out the bed light. The telephone goes on ringing. In the dark*) I love you, Sally.

SALLY

No. No, don't say that. You mustn't. We must keep this gay!

(*The telephone goes on ringing.*)

CURTAIN

Act Three

ACT THREE

Scene I

Scene: *The same. Noon. Sunday.*
When the curtain rises, a card-table has been set up and laid for breakfast for two. SALLY'S *bed has been made; the day-bed is still turned down and unslept in, as it was left. In the bedroom,* BILL'S *coat and cap are on the back of a chair.*

In the kitchen, breakfast is cooking—coffee on the stove, and water boiling in a saucepan. SALLY *comes through into the living room with two glasses of orange juice, which she puts on the table, attending to the toaster and starting to pour the coffee which she also fetches from the kitchen.* BILL *comes into the bedroom from the bathroom, fully dressed, except for his coat.*

BILL
(*Calling*)
How's everything coming?

SALLY
(*Calling back*)
Everything's ready!
(BILL *puts on his coat, tossing his cap onto the bed, and goes into the living room.*)

BILL
Oh, boy, sumpn' smells good!

SALLY

It's the coffee. I wish coffee tasted as good as it smells.

BILL

I think if I were a woman, I'd *wear* coffee as a perfume. (*He kisses her and then, feeling thoroughly at home, removes his coat and throws it across the back of the couch.*)

SALLY

(*Rising*)

I'll just see if the water's boiling for the eggs.

BILL

No, don't. Sit down. Be still. There's lots of time for the eggs.

SALLY

But the water will boil over.

BILL

No, it won't. Unless you've overfilled the saucepan. It'll just boil away. And I suppose that'll worry you. Mustn't leave the water alone. It'll get hurt.

SALLY

(*Smiling*)

I'd better turn it off. (*Goes into kitchen*) Don't you *want* eggs? I can just as easily put them on.

BILL

And then keep hopping up and down, watching the time? No, let's have our coffee in peace.

SALLY

All right. (*She turns off the stove and comes back to living room, where she takes the toast from the toaster, bringing it to the table.*)

BILL

(*Rising*)

One thing *I'll* do before we really settle.

SALLY

What's that?

BILL

Cover up the day-bed. Don't you think it looks kind of . . . deserted and reproachful . . . all unslept in?

SALLY

(*Helping him with the cover*)

Yes, I do. I always think a bed that hasn't been slept in looks sort of forlorn in the morning. If ever I come in very late at night, and my bed's been turned down, I always want to say to it, "It's all right. Here I am."

BILL

(*Straightening the cover*)

Do you have a Sunday paper?

SALLY

(*Returning to the table*)

No, we'll have to go out for one. We should have thought of it last night.

BILL

I'll go and get it, later. I must have my funnies.

SALLY

Me, too. It wouldn't be Sunday to me, without Dick Tracy.

BILL

Let's get *all* the Sunday papers, and really mess up the apartment. (*Comes back to the table and sits*) This is so pleasant, Sally *dear*. Our second breakfast together. Quite an old married couple. You're nice to have breakfast with.

SALLY

So are you. Have you . . . have you had breakfast with a lot of girls?

BILL

(*Putting down his cup*)

Sally, that is not a question to ask *now*. If ever.

SALLY

I wasn't being curious . . . about your life, I mean. I was just wondering whether there was a lot of difference between girls at breakfast.

BILL

Yes. Quite a lot.

SALLY

Do some of them . . . bother you . . . *talking* about things?

BILL

Sally, stop it.

SALLY

I'm asking quite impersonally.

118

BILL

You can't. It's an extremely personal question.

SALLY

I'm sorry. There ought to be a book of rules for conversation on occasions like this.

BILL

There oughtn't to be a book at all. Just be natural, and yourself.

SALLY

I *was* being myself.

BILL

Well, then, *don't* be yourself. Think of the other fellow for a change.

SALLY

I didn't mean . . .

BILL

Sally, I said "stop."

SALLY

I'm sorry. Shall I start some more toast?

BILL

Yes, please, unless it means fetching it from the kitchen.

SALLY

No, I've got it right here.

BILL

Then, yes, please.
(*She rises. The front-door buzzer goes. They both start.*)

SALLY

(*In a stricken whisper*)

Olive!

BILL

(*Also whispering*)

Don't answer it.

SALLY

(*Whispering*)

Oh, but I must!

BILL

(*Whispering*)

Let her think you've gone out. She'll go away.

SALLY

(*Still whispering*)

She'll ask the elevator man, and he'll tell her I haven't. She'll come back.

BILL

Let her.

SALLY

I can't. I'll get rid of her. You go into the bathroom. (*She starts him toward bathroom.*)

BILL

And suppose *she* wants to go to the bathroom?

SALLY

Then go into the kitchen. Take all that with you. (*Indicating table.*)

BILL

Really!
(*The buzzer sounds again.*)

SALLY

(*Whispering feverishly*)

Please!
(BILL *unwillingly takes the table and carries it through to the kitchen.* SALLY *follows with the toaster. Then she looks around, straightening the chairs. The buzzer goes again.*)

SALLY

(*Calling*)

I'm just coming! (*She starts for the door, and then remembers* BILL's *coat, lying over the back of the couch. She gets that, too, and thrusts it at him in the kitchen. Then, in a wild scramble, she opens the door.* OLIVE *is outside.*)

SALLY

(*With creditable surprise*)

Olive!

OLIVE

I've been ringing and ringing.

SALLY

I'm sorry. I was in the bathroom. I *thought* I heard the buzzer.
(*Throughout the ensuing scene,* BILL *is in the kitchen, listening and pantomiming reactions to what goes on, while he puts on his coat and drinks the remainder of his coffee.*)

OLIVE

Well, how are you this morning?

SALLY

(*Wandering around, looking for traces of* BILL *to cover*)
I'm fine.

OLIVE

You were out very late last night.

SALLY

I know. (*Then, quickly*) How do *you* know?

OLIVE

I called you until three o'clock. What time did you get in?

SALLY

Oh, about . . . a quarter past, I think.

OLIVE

Where did you go?

SALLY

(*Still wandering*)
To the Persian Room with Ken.

OLIVE

Ken? Bartlett? Are you and he on again?

SALLY

Oh, no. We met at the theatre. What did you call up for?

OLIVE

I wanted to talk to you. Why did you and Bill cut me last night?

SALLY

(*Indignant and stopping her walk*)

We didn't. We waved and waved. You saw us. You waved back.

OLIVE

I mean in the intermission. I looked for you everywhere.

SALLY

We went next door for a drink with Ken. (*She starts to prowl again, tidying things.*)

OLIVE

How did you get tickets? Ned had to pay $17.60 each for the twenty-seventh row or something. You were way down front.

SALLY

(*Straightening the cover on the day-bed*)

Ken gave us the house seats.

OLIVE

What *are* you fidgeting around like that for? Come and sit down, for goodness' sake.

SALLY

I'm sorry. (*She picks up the evening paper lying on the desk, and suddenly remembers that this is where* BILL'*s cap has formerly been. She wonders where it is and then, with a glance at the bedroom, remembers with a gasp.*)

123

OLIVE

(*Noticing the gasp*)

What's the matter?

SALLY

Nothing. Why?

OLIVE

The way you jumped.

SALLY

(*Innocently*)

I just remembered something.

OLIVE

What?

SALLY

Something I've got to do. Listen, is that the telephone?

OLIVE

I don't hear anything.

SALLY

I think it is. I'll just go see. (*She goes into the bedroom, picks the cap up quickly, goes to the night table, stuffs it into the drawer, looks around again and then picks up the telephone.*) Hello? Hello? No, I guess it wasn't. (*She returns to the living room.*)

OLIVE

Well, then, now will you sit down and relax?

SALLY

Yes, now I'll sit down and relax. (*She does so.*)

OLIVE

You and Bill have certainly been seeing a lot of each other!

SALLY

Well, I don't think he knows many people in New York.

OLIVE

(*Sarcastically*)

So you thought you'd be kind to him.

SALLY

(*Sharply*)

It wasn't a question of being kind to him. He's very nice. Very nice indeed. (*She turns her head slightly toward kitchen, where* BILL *pantomimes his reaction to this.*)

OLIVE

I know he is. I introduced him to you. Where did he finally end up staying?

SALLY

He got a room at the Hotel Taft.

OLIVE

Is he there now, do you know?

SALLY

How should I know?

OLIVE

Would you mind if I called him up?

SALLY

No, of course not.

OLIVE

(*Starting across to bedroom. Stops in doorway*)

Come and talk to me.

(SALLY, *who has made a small start toward kitchen, follows her.* BILL *applies his eye to the door crack and sees them go. He waits a moment, and then takes the opportunity to slip out. He makes for the front door, looks around for his cap, remembers where it is, gives a panic-stricken look at the bedroom, and then shrugs his shoulders and slips out. In the meantime, in the bedroom, the following scene takes place.*)

OLIVE

Where's the book? (*She puts her hand to the night-table drawer.*)

SALLY

(*Hastily*)

It's underneath . . . on the floor.

OLIVE

Oh, yes. You are nervous this morning.

SALLY

(*Sitting on bed*)

I'm sorry.

OLIVE

(*Hunting for the number*)

What did you think of the show last night?

SALLY

I thought it was lovely.

OLIVE

I thought it stank.

SALLY

Oh . . . why?

OLIVE

What do you mean—why?

SALLY

I mean—why?

OLIVE

(*Crossly*)

I don't know why. I thought it did. If I tell you a piece of fish stinks, you don't ask me why, do you? (*Dials number.*)

SALLY

It's a big hit.

OLIVE

Anything's a hit in war time.

SALLY

Not the plays I'm in. Oh . . .

OLIVE

(*Into phone*)

I want to speak to Sergeant Page, please. Oh, all right. (*To* SALLY) What were you going to say?

SALLY

I've got a job.

OLIVE

You haven't! What? (*Into phone*) I want to speak to Sergeant Page, please. Sergeant William Page. Yes, he's registered there. (*To* SALLY) What's the job?

SALLY

They've let Myra Foley out of *The Dark Dreamer*. They sent for me yesterday.

OLIVE

Darling, how exciting! I hear it's a wonderful part. (*Flatly*) I had an offer yesterday, too.

SALLY

Oh, what was it?

OLIVE

(*Grimly*)

They want me to go out with *Tobacco Road!*

SALLY

Are you going?

OLIVE

Darling . . . all those turnips? (*Into phone*) Oh . . . well, will you say Miss Lashbrooke called? Lashbrooke. L-A-S—No, S as in . . . Oh, hell, say Olive. Yes, Olive. (*Hangs up*) Not there.

SALLY

He's probably gone out.

128

OLIVE

Aren't you smart?

SALLY

Olive, don't be that way. What's the matter?

OLIVE

(*Turning on her*)

The matter is that I don't like the way you've acted over Bill. He was my beau, and . . .

SALLY

And you left him on my hands.

OLIVE

Not for you to take over.

SALLY

I haven't "taken him over."

OLIVE

I thought I was safe with *you*.

SALLY

Well, I like that. Why?

OLIVE

I thought you were all broken up about Kenneth Bartlett. I should have known that was just the dangerous time. (*She goes into the living room.*)

SALLY

(*Following her*)

What was I to do? Leave him alone all week-end?

129

OLIVE

That wasn't your business.

SALLY

You turned him down for your Commander friend. What's happened to him, by the way?

OLIVE

He had to go call on his grandmother in Gramercy Park. We're meeting for lunch at the Brevoort.

SALLY

You've been having fun this week-end. Why shouldn't I?

OLIVE

Did you say *fun?*

SALLY

Hasn't it been?

OLIVE

You went to the Persian Room last night. What do you think *we* did?

SALLY

What?

OLIVE

Played gin rummy at the 1-2-3 until four o'clock, when he practically passed out from Cubre Libres. He's only just *discovered* gin rummy. That's the kind of guy he is. I think the real reason I hated the show so much last night was that he worshipped it. And so noisily.

SALLY

Yes, I heard his laugh.

130

OLIVE

It stopped the show in one place. The whole audience turned around. Of course, I know he's good-looking. . . .

SALLY

(*Involuntarily*)

Oh . . . (*She stops.*)

OLIVE

What were you going to say?

SALLY

I was sort of . . . disappointed in his looks.

OLIVE

Oh, no, he's *terribly* good-looking. Although the hairline did seem to me to have receded a little since last year. And to think I passed up Bill for that! What time's Bill going back tonight—do you know?

SALLY

No, I don't.

OLIVE

Maybe we could dine together. If not, let's you and me. Dutch.

SALLY

I . . . I don't think I can.

OLIVE

Why? What are you doing?

SALLY

I've got to work on the part.

OLIVE

Just an early dinner. I'd like to get to bed early, anyway.

SALLY

(*Rising*)

We'll see, but I don't think so. Thank you very much.

OLIVE

Now *you*'re mad at *me!*

SALLY

Well, I don't think you've any right . . .

OLIVE

(*Rising*)

I have a perfect right. Bill was *my* gink.

SALLY

(*Courageously for a second*)

Well, he isn't any more!

OLIVE

You know, I'm a fool. That's what's the matter with me. Trusting everyone! Gullible Gertie! You . . . who were so worried about yourself the other afternoon . . . who were going to "give it all up" . . .

SALLY

Well, I meant that . . .

OLIVE

(*Rising*)

Only Bill came along, and you couldn't keep your hands off him.

SALLY

(*Angry, and also agonized, imagining that* BILL *can hear*)
Olive . . . I think you'd better go!

OLIVE

Oh, I'll go fast enough, only . . . (*The telephone rings. They both start*) There's your telephone.
(SALLY *goes into the bedroom and answers it.*)

SALLY

Hello . . . yes . . . Who's that? (*Her mouth opens in astonishment. She looks involuntarily toward the kitchen*) Where are you? How did you . . . ? (*She smiles*) Yes . . . yes, of course you can come around. Olive's here. She's just been calling you at the Taft.

OLIVE

(*Coming into the room*)
Let me talk to him.

SALLY

She wants to talk to you. . . . Yes, as soon as you like. Yes, I know. I've got it. *No!* All right. Here. Here's Olive. (*She hands the phone to* OLIVE.)

OLIVE

(*Cooing a little*)
Bill? How are you? I've been calling and calling you. What are you doing? How soon? (*Looks at her watch*) Well, don't make it any more. I've got to run. I'll see you. (*She hangs up*) Where was he?

SALLY

At a drug store.

OLIVE

Where—did he say?

SALLY

He said quite near.

OLIVE

I'll just wait and say hello to him.

SALLY

What time is your lunch?

OLIVE

One.

SALLY

It must be almost that now.

OLIVE

He can wait. (*Honeyedly*) What were we talking about?

SALLY

(*Primly*)

I think I'd asked you to go, and you said you would.

OLIVE

Oh, darling, you didn't mean that. Nor did I. (*She kisses her.*)

SALLY

(*With distaste*)

Let's go in the other room. Oh . . . (*She pauses.*)

OLIVE

What is it?

SALLY

Just . . . the thing I remembered before. Something I have to give the elevator man. You go on. I'll be right after you. (*She moves toward the dressing room, as though she were going in, to deceive* OLIVE. OLIVE *goes on into the living room, where she sees the manuscript on a table, and picks it up to read.* SALLY *takes* BILL's *cap from the drawer of the night table and looks around for something to wrap it in. All there is is a copy of* Vogue. *She thrusts it between the pages, and goes out to the front door.*)

OLIVE

What have you got there?

SALLY

Just a copy of *Vogue*.

OLIVE

What does the elevator man want a copy of *Vogue* for?

SALLY

(*Opening the door*)

For his wife.

OLIVE

Really! You don't mind my looking at your script?

SALLY

(*As she goes*)

No, of course not. (*She goes out, leaving the door open.* OLIVE *sits puzzledly with the script, not looking at it.* SALLY *returns from elevator, smiling contentedly.*)

135

OLIVE

(*Suspiciously*)

You're very pleased with yourself about something.

SALLY

(*Airily*)

No, no. I'm just happy.

OLIVE

What about?

SALLY

(*Vaguely*)

Oh . . . everything.

OLIVE

(*After a moment's scrutiny of her*)

Sally . . . you wouldn't be going and getting silly and sentimental over Bill, would you? Because, if you do, you'll lose him
even quicker than you lost Kenneth Bartlett.

SALLY

I've no intention of getting sentimental.

OLIVE

(*Sweetly*)

No, darling, no intention—but you're the kind who can't sew
a button on for a man without thinking it's for life. And Bill's
told me, over and over again, that he's no place for sentiment in
his scheme of things.

SALLY

(*After a silence, rising*)

Well, I've told you before, neither have I . . . any more. So
that's all right. (*Doorbell rings*) There he is.

OLIVE

He's got here quick.
>   (SALLY *opens door. Enter* BILL. *He wears his cap, carries
>   the Sunday newspaper, and some flowers in paper.*)

BILL

>   (*Gesturing with his cap*)

Hello.

SALLY

>   (*Smiling broadly*)

Hello.

OLIVE

Hello, Bill.

BILL

>   (*Pleasantly, but perfunctorily*)

Hello. (*To* SALLY) I was afraid I might be calling too early
for you, but I had to go out to get my Sunday paper, so I brought
you these. (*He hands her the flowers.*)

SALLY

Oh . . . how lovely! (*She looks at them*) "Daffodils . . .
that come before the swallow dares . . ."

BILL

>   (*Finishing the quotation*)

"And take the winds of March with beauty."

OLIVE

What a cute saying!

137

BILL

He was a cute sayer.

OLIVE

Who?

BILL

Shakespeare.

SALLY

I love spring flowers. Thank you so much. I'll just put them in water. (*She takes them to the kitchen.*)

BILL

Well, what sort of a time have *you* been having?

OLIVE

Not a lot of fun. What time do you have to go back tonight?

BILL

Around ten.

OLIVE

Well, Ned's train goes at four. I wonder . . . could we dine together?

BILL

I'm afraid I have a dinner date.

OLIVE

Oh, that's too bad. Well, maybe a cocktail?

BILL

I'm afraid that's gone, too.

138

OLIVE

(*Defeated*)

Oh. Oh, well, I'm sorry. (*Telephone rings*) There's the telephone. Sally! Sally! Telephone!

SALLY

(*Coming from kitchen*)

I know. I heard it. (*She goes through to the bedroom, leaving the door open.*)

OLIVE

I have to go. I'll just wait until Sally's through. (*She starts to put on her gloves.*)

SALLY

(*Into telephone*)

Hello? Yes . . . Well, I . . . You have? Oh, how wonderful! Where? Yes . . . yes, of course. Right away. (*She hangs up, stands a moment, bothered, and then returns to the living room.*)

SALLY

I've got to go out.

BILL

(*Disappointed*)

Oh . . . where?

SALLY

That was the producer calling. They've made another change in the cast. The leading man's out, and they've got Henry Atherton! (OLIVE *pulls a face*) He was the star of Olive's show that just closed.

BILL

Yes, I know. He was the one with the . . . (*He indicates his hair*) Yes, I remember.

SALLY

They want me to go and work with him this afternoon.

BILL

Could you lunch with me first?

SALLY

I'm afraid I can't. I've got to go right away. *They*'ve all had big breakfasts.

BILL

Well, can I take you there?

SALLY

(*Nodding*)

I'll just go and change. (*She runs back to the bedroom, closing the door behind her, and disappears into the dressing-room.*)

OLIVE

(*Sugaredly*)

Sally's sweet, isn't she?

BILL

She certainly is.

OLIVE

But, you know, playing with Henry Atherton, I'm afraid she's headed for trouble. She's just about the age he likes them.

BILL

Oh, I should think Sally could take care of herself.

OLIVE

Oh, yes, she can . . . if she wants to. But a star's a star, and she's always had a crush on him. (*Collecting herself to go*) Can you still not manage cocktails, by the way?

BILL

I'm afraid I can't.

OLIVE

Well, you'll let me know next time you're coming, wont you? And . . . (*Seductively*) I won't let *anything* interfere.

BILL

Olive, I'm afraid I don't play around with married women.

OLIVE

(*After a defeated second*)

Oh, but that's all over. We talked it out thoroughly. I'm not seeing him again.

BILL

You mean—you're divorcing?

OLIVE

Yes.

BILL

Do you think that looks well—to divorce a service man?

OLIVE

Just what are you trying to say?

BILL

Just . . . very tactfully, and with no hard feelings . . . that I think we'd better . . . leave things as they are.

OLIVE

(*Rallying after a moment*)

I guess I bought that all right! Well, I've got to lunch with my ex. Good-bye, Bill.

BILL

Good-bye, Olive.
     (*They shake hands.*)

OLIVE

Say good-bye to Sally for me. (*She turns at the door*) By the way, did Sally *tell* you anything about Ned?

BILL

No. But I saw him with you last night. And, Olive, you'd never have married that—not in a million years.

OLIVE

(*Looking at him*)

I never knew men could be such bitches! (*She goes.*)
     (BILL *laughs, takes a cigarette.* SALLY *returns in a hurry, having changed her dress and carrying her hat, bag, gloves and shoes.*)

SALLY

Has she gone?

BILL

She's gone. I'm afraid that's the end of a beautiful friendship.

SALLY

(*Putting on her shoes*)

I'm afraid . . . for *me*, too.

BILL

Well, it can't be helped. Where are you rehearsing?

SALLY

At Henry Atherton's apartment. It's on 90th Street.

BILL

Is that usual?

SALLY

What?

BILL

Rehearsing in actors' apartments?

SALLY

Oh . . . yes . . . quite. If they're stars.

BILL

Is anyone else going to be there?

SALLY

I guess so. Why—what's the matter?

BILL

(*Briefly*)

Nothing. (*Changing his mood*) How long will it go on?

SALLY

All afternoon, I'm afraid.

BILL

(*Lightly*)

What am *I* going to do?

SALLY

Would you like to come back here? I'll give you the key, and you can . . . use the apartment as if it were your own.

BILL

I thought that's what I *had* been doing. You'll have dinner with me?

SALLY

Yes.

BILL

Promise?

SALLY

I promise. Now I must go.

BILL

(*Stopping her and holding her*)

Sally, I don't see anything of you . . . at all! I want to talk to you . . . about so many things.

144

SALLY

(Shying)

No—why? We don't need to talk. There's nothing to talk about. We've had a lovely time, and . . . well, we don't want to get . . . sentimental about it. Do we?

BILL

(Quietly—disappointed)

I guess not.

SALLY

Well, then. Come along. I'm late. (*She goes to the door. He stands still. She looks back at him*) Aren't you coming?

BILL

(After a second)

Sure.

SALLY

I'll just ring for the elevator.
> (*She goes out. He looks after her a moment, putting out his cigarette, his face puzzled and unhappy. Then he picks up his cap, shrugs, and follows her out.*)

CURTAIN

ACT THREE

Scene II

SCENE: *The same. About six-thirty.*

The card-table is set up again, laid now for supper. The whole room has been made to look as attractive as possible. The daffodils are in a vase, and there are a number of other vases of spring flowers, including some sprays of white lilac.

BILL *is kneeling on the day-bed, a book in his hand, dividing his attention between it and the window from which he is watching for* SALLY's *return. After a moment, he sees her coming, goes into the kitchen, opens the icebox and takes out a bottle of champagne, which he brings to the living room, setting it on a side-table, where two champagne glasses are waiting. Then the buzzer sounds, and he goes to the door and opens it.* SALLY *is outside.*

SALLY

(Subduedly)

Hi!

BILL

Hi!

SALLY

(Seeing the table)

Why, what's all this?

BILL

I thought we'd have dinner home tonight.

146

SALLY

It'll be rather a picnic one.

BILL

Well . . .

SALLY

Lunch sausage and marinated herring, I'm afraid.

BILL

That's all right.

SALLY

Where did these flowers come from? (*She turns, looking around*) Oh, but all these . . . Bill, you shouldn't!

BILL

You said you liked spring flowers, and the streets were full of them.

SALLY

Oh, but they're beautiful. (*She goes from vase to vase*) The whole room smells of them. I've never had so many. Bill, you darling . . . (*She goes to him impulsively and kisses him. Then she retreats, subduedly*) Thank you *so* much.

BILL

(*Slightly constrained, too*)

How about a drink?

SALLY

(*Seeing the tray*)

Champagne? Where did you find that?

BILL

(*Opening the bottle*)

I found it.

SALLY

Not in *my* wine cellar!

BILL

Like some?

SALLY

Yes, please! Oh, Bill, this is very nice.

BILL

I'm glad you're pleased.

SALLY

(*Sitting on the couch*)

It's the loveliest spring evening out.

BILL

I know. I've been looking at it, watching for you to come back.

SALLY

You know, two days ago . . . the day you got here . . . it was still all grim and wintry . . . and suddenly since then it's come with a rush. Sometimes I feel that I can't bear the spring, it's so exciting!

BILL

(*Handing her a glass*)

I know. I walked in the Park after I left you, and it's bursting all over it. All the trees and shrubs in a kind of young green haze, and all the flowers on the corner stands looked as if they were growing there, and you wanted to buy great armfuls . . .

SALLY

You *did* buy great armfuls.

BILL

I bought all I could carry. (*Lifting his glass*) Well . . . to the spring.

SALLY

The spring.
    (*They drink.*)

BILL

(*Affecting casualness*)
How was the rehearsal?

SALLY

That was exciting, too.

BILL

And Henry Atherton?

SALLY

He was good. You're right, though. It *is* dyed. But he's going to be wonderful in it. I don't know . . . I daren't say it yet . . . but I really think that this may be what I've been waiting for all these years.

BILL

(*With slight double meaning*)
This . . . play, you mean?

SALLY

(*Not getting it*)

Yes. Perhaps that's part of the spring, too.

BILL

(*In a new voice*)

Sally . . .

SALLY

What?

BILL

(*Sitting beside her*)

This is . . . *our* spring, isn't it? We'll have it together?

SALLY

(*A little evasive*)

Of course . . . if you're going to be here.

BILL

I think I am. I think I can count on the spring and summer . . . if I'm lucky. I've been thinking of it all afternoon. Things that we can do together.

SALLY

(*Smiling nervously and taking a cigarette*)

Give me a light.

BILL

(*Taking the cigarette from her*)

Sally, don't do that.

SALLY

What?

BILL

Hold out on me.

SALLY

I don't know what you mean.

BILL

I wanted us to have dinner here tonight, because . . . well, partly because I wanted to talk to you . . .

SALLY

I wish you wouldn't.

BILL

Sally . . . if I told you that . . . given the least possible encouragement from you . . . I think I could be . . . very much in love with you . . . what would you say?

SALLY

(*After a second*)

I wouldn't give it to you.

BILL

Why not?

SALLY

Because I don't want you to be in love with me . . . or think you are.

BILL

Why don't you?

SALLY

Because . . . that isn't how we started this.

BILL

Sally, you don't go into a love affair *deliberately* . . .

SALLY

I know, but . . . I don't want it to *be* like that. This way it's
. . . fun.

BILL

Will it be any less fun if I'm in love with you?

SALLY

(*Positively*)

Oh . . . *yes!* Bill, we don't have to talk about it. It *has* been
fun . . . it *is* fun . . . it can go on being fun, if you won't spoil it.

BILL

That is a remark I seem to have heard before . . . but not
from anyone like you.

SALLY

What do you mean?

BILL

It's the kind of thing old-fashioned women used to say . . .
the older, married women . . . when they wanted to keep you
hanging around.

SALLY

But I do want to keep you . . . well, not *hanging* around . . .
but *around* . . . if you want to be.

152

BILL

I do.

SALLY

Well, then . . . (*She moves away.*)

BILL

(*After a moment*)

I can't be so crazy as to have got you *all* wrong, but . . . you baffle me, Sally.

SALLY

I don't see why.

BILL

I guess it's the times.

SALLY

(*Puzzled*)

The *Times?*

BILL

I don't mean the newspaper. I mean . . . the times . . . the war, or something. Or perhaps it's the theatre.

SALLY

I still don't know what you're talking about.

BILL

(*Rising and going to her*)

Sally, you're not the kind of girl who has affairs . . . promiscuously . . . Or are you?

SALLY

I don't know.

BILL

What do you mean?

SALLY

I mean, I don't know what constitutes "promiscuously." I have affairs. I mean, I've *had* affairs.

BILL

(*Quietly*)

Many affairs?

SALLY

You told me that was a question that one shouldn't ask.

BILL

I was quite right. One shouldn't. But, Sally, if I said that rather than keep this . . . just an affair . . . I'd sooner . . . call the whole thing off—what would you say?

SALLY

(*After a long pause*)

I think I'd say . . . we'd better call it off.

BILL

Are you afraid of getting hurt?

SALLY

Maybe.

BILL

Sally, I wouldn't hurt you.

154

SALLY

That's something that I don't see how anyone can promise anyone . . . ever. And I wish you wouldn't talk about it.

BILL

There was a book of poems by your bed . . . (*Fetching it from the day-bed*) Poems by Dorothy Parker. You had a whole lot of them marked. Why did you have them marked?

SALLY

I guess . . . because I liked them.

BILL

This one . . . (*He finds it and reads*)
>   *"I will not make you songs of hearts denied,*
>   *And you, being man, would have no tears of me,*
>   *And should I offer you fidelity*
>   *You'd be, I think, a little terrified."*
(*He closes the book*) That one's *double*-marked. You must have liked it a lot.

SALLY

I do.

BILL

Was that, by any chance, your experience with Kenneth Bartlett?

SALLY

Perhaps . . . a little.

BILL

And you're afraid of it happening again?

SALLY

It always happens . . . doesn't it?

BILL

I don't think so.

SALLY

Well, it always does to me.

BILL

Always?

SALLY

Yes, always.

BILL

(*Gently*)

How *often* has it happened to you?

SALLY

Twice. So far.

BILL

(*Smiling, relieved*)

Is that all?

SALLY

What do you mean?

BILL

Is that all the affairs you've had? Two?

SALLY

(*Turning to him—with naive pleasure*)

You don't think that a lot?

156

BILL

No. Though I think it's two too many . . . for *you*.

SALLY

How many have *you* had?

BILL

I've never counted. And if I had, I wouldn't tell you.

SALLY

I told *you*.

BILL

I know.

SALLY

(*With tiny sarcasm*)

You think it's different for a man?

BILL

I think the permissible *number* is different for a man.

SALLY

You knew about me, didn't you? You didn't believe that story about the pajamas?

BILL

No.

SALLY

Well, then . . .

BILL

Yes . . . but, Sally, I want this to have *meant* something to you.

157

SALLY

It did. It was terribly sweet . . .

BILL

But that's all? You won't let it mean more? Not even if I tell you that . . . if you offered me fidelity, I'd be . . . I think . . . a little *gratified?* In fact, that if you *don't* offer it to me, I'll feel as if I'd had a door slammed right bang in my face.

SALLY

(*Moved, protesting*)

Oh, Bill!

BILL

As if the spring had suddenly turned around and said, "That's all there is. Now you can go back to winter."

SALLY

Not winter. We can keep it spring.

BILL

Nothing *stays* spring. And I wouldn't want it to. There'd be something stultified and horrible about the spring, if it always stayed like that. It's *got* to become summer, and fall, and . . .

SALLY

(*Bitterly*)

Winter.

BILL

Yes, one day. But for both of us . . . at the same time. Sally, I *am* in love with you. There's still time to turn back . . . for me to turn back, I mean . . . without it's hurting too much. I told you

I didn't believe in being unhappily in love. I don't. And I'm not going to be. I'm not having an awfully happy time right now. None of us are. That's not a bid for pity. It's just telling you why I feel this way. I gave up looking forward to anything seven years ago, and I've got along all right that way. With . . . Olive . . . and taking what came. That's how I wanted it. And I can go on like that. But I can't begin again . . . hoping . . . and wanting . . . and planning . . . unless there is *some* chance of those plans working out. *You're* scared of getting hurt again. Well, so am I. *Bitterly* scared.

SALLY

(*Almost in tears*)

What do you *want?*

BILL

(*Beside her now*)

I want you to let yourself love me . . . if you *can*. Because I think you can. I think you've a great talent for love, Sally, and that you're trying to fritter it and dissipate it . . . because it's been trodden on before. And if you go on like that, you'll kill it. And . . . (*Slowly*) I think that's one talent that *is* death to hide. (SALLY *bursts into tears*) Yes, cry, if you want to. Please, please cry. Only . . . don't shut me out . . . and don't shut yourself out.

SALLY

(*Sobbing*)

Oh, Bill . . .

BILL

I'm not asking such a great deal. I think I'd like to marry you, but we won't talk of *that*, yet. I want you to love me . . . *terribly*, but I'm not even asking *that* of you, yet.

SALLY

(*Between tears*)

I do love you! I love you terribly! That's the hell of it!
(*Scrambling to her knees on the couch beside him*) I won't make
scenes, Bill. I won't be troublesome. . . .

BILL

(*Taking her face in his hands*)

Ssh. You've said all I wanted you to say now. (*He kisses her
gently*) Drink up your drink. It's getting warm.

SALLY

(*Gulping it and tears at the same time*)

I shall be tight again. I haven't had any food.

BILL

What—not all day? Well, then, you must have dinner right
away. Come and sit down.

SALLY

It'll take a little while to fix.

BILL

It's all fixed. They're sending it up from next door. From
. . . "our" place. It's coming up at seven. The first course is in
the icebox. Vichysoisse. I'll get it right now. (*He starts to the
kitchen.*)

SALLY

Bill . . . (*She moves toward him.*)

160

BILL

(*At kitchen door*)

You pour yourself another drink and sit down. Pour me one, too. (*He goes into the kitchen and takes two cups of soup from the icebox.* SALLY, *moving a little as if in a dream, refills the glasses and brings them to the table, where she sits.* BILL *returns and places the soup*) There. (*He bends and kisses her lightly on the top of her head. Then, standing waiter-like, with his napkin over his arm*) Madame est servie. (*He sits.* SALLY *is still blinking away tears. She dips a spoon, and tastes.*)

SALLY

Oh, Bill, this is heaven.

BILL

(*Who hasn't touched his—looking at her*)

Isn't it? (*He puts out his hand, and holds hers. They look at each other and smile, and then, still holding hands, dip their spoons and begin to eat.*)

CURTAIN